What People Are Saying about
Longing

In *Longing* Chris Sansone provides us with a roadmap home to our one, true Self—the one being each of us is but most of us have forgotten. To awaken to and live as the Self is the highest purpose an incarnation in the Earth School can serve. In this beautiful book, Chris takes your hand and, if you will but allow it, gently and lovingly guides you Home.
Robert Schwartz, Between Lives Soul Regression hypnotist and author of *Your Soul's Plan, Your Soul's Gift,* and *Your Soul's Love*

Longing: A Pilgrimage to the Quiet Power Within is a profound and transformative journey into the depths of the human soul. Christopher Sansone beautifully illuminates the universal longing we all feel—a yearning for connection, meaning, and purpose—and shows us how to find that quiet power within ourselves. His work resonates deeply with my own longing to living a committed life, as he guides readers to align with their highest truth and contribute to evolutionary purpose. This book is for anyone seeking healing, fulfillment, and a life of profound love and impact.
Lynne Twist, best-selling author of *The Soul of Money: Transforming Your Relationship with Money and Life* and *Living a Committed Life: Finding Freedom and Fulfillment in a Purpose Larger Than Yourself*

This stands out as an accessible self-help spiritual book that gives the reader guideposts for their inner quest to transform. Chris weaves his journey of personal wisdom with his expert knowledge, uniquely blending psychology with Hindu gems and other spiritual teachings. He documents the path from

shame and loneliness to spiritual awareness—a process he calls 'soul genius.' Five stories make the transformational steps come alive.
Annabelle Nelson, PhD, Professor at the Fielding Graduate University and author of *Archetypal Imagery and the Spiritual Self: Techniques for Coaches and Therapists.*

Longing is a deeply inspiring book that invites you to awaken to your innate wisdom and wholeness. Christopher Sansone seamlessly weaves together insight from wisdom traditions, research, and lived experiences, offering profound teachings for living your life's purpose. From intergenerational trauma to the elusive nature of shame, this book will help you sort through anything that does not align with your true nature so that you may rest in the infinite truth of who you are.
Harmony Kwiker, MA, LPC, author of *Align: Living and Loving from the True Self*

This book offers a reflective exploration of the soul's longing as a sacred guide for healing and transformation. Similar in many respects to a shamanic or hero's journey, it shows how skillful responding to inner yearning can open the door to spiritual wisdom and the unseen realms. The integration of psychological insight and spiritual depth offers a grounded yet transcendent approach, inviting each reader to awaken their quiet power within and embark on a journey of profound healing.
Nita Gage, DSPS, MA, author of *Soul Whispering: The Art of Awakening Shamanic Consciousness* and *Women in Storage: How to Reimagine Your Life*

A must-read for anyone seeking to deepen their spiritual understanding, heal generational wounds, and live authentically with compassion and purpose. It is a powerful companion for those ready to embrace their inner truth and find peace within their personal journey.

Kelly Bearer, MA, LPCC, ACHT Founder, Boulder Hypnotherapy Institute

those ready to embrace their inner truth and find peace within their personal journey.
Kelly Bearer, MA, LPCC, ACHT Founder, Boulder Hypnotherapy Institute

Longing

A Pilgrimage to Your Quiet Power Within

Longing

A Pilgrimage to Your Quiet Power Within

Christopher Sansone, PhD, CPCC

MANTRA
BOOKS

London, UK
Washington, DC, USA

CollectiveInk

First published by Mantra Books, 2026
Mantra Books is an imprint of Collective Ink Ltd.,
Unit 11, Shepperton House, 89 Shepperton Road, London, N1 3DF
office@collectiveinkbooks.com
www.collectiveinkbooks.com
www.mantra-books.net

For distributor details and how to order please visit the 'Ordering' section on our website.

Text copyright: Christopher Sansone, PhD 2025

ISBN: 978 1 917704 39 7
978 1 917704 42 7 (ebook)
Library of Congress Control Number: 2025906642

All rights reserved. Except for brief quotations in critical articles or reviews, no part of this book may be reproduced in any manner without prior written permission from the publishers.

The rights of Christopher Sansone, PhD as author have been asserted in accordance with the Copyright, Designs and Patents Act 1988.

A CIP catalogue record for this book is available from the British Library.

Design: Lapiz Digital Services

UK: Printed and bound by CPI Group (UK) Ltd, Croydon, CR0 4YY
Printed in North America by CPI GPS partners

The manufacturer's authorised representative in the EU for product safety is:
eucomply OÜ – Pärnu mnt 139b-14, 11317 Tallinn, Estonia, hello@ eucompliancepartner.com,
www.eucompliancepartner.com

We operate a distinctive and ethical publishing philosophy in all areas of our business, from our global network of authors to production and worldwide distribution.

*To the healers among us and the guides with us
To my life-loving, spirit-rich, life partner, Maria
To my children Kellen, Andrew, and Carina living
and becoming their unique selves has opened me to
my better versions*

*To Mom
To Dad*

We, pilgrims on Earth,
though must find our way,
never travel alone.

Contents

Acknowledgments	xiii
Introduction	xv
Chapter One: The Wound and the Lie	1
Chapter Two: Irony of Shame	11
Chapter Three: Pilgrimage of Longing	17
Chapter Four: Soul Healing	24
Chapter Five: Kosha Power	33
Chapter Six: Vitalities and Realities	50
Chapter Seven: Omega Point	58
Chapter Eight: Living Transformations	66
Chapter Nine: What Heroes Know	105
Chapter Ten: By Love's Way	114
Chapter Eleven: In Stillness	135
Chapter Twelve: In Forgiving	145
Chapter Thirteen: Soul Genius	155
Chapter Fourteen: Waves of Light	161
About the Author	167
References	169

Acknowledgments

Writing this book has often felt like hiking a long, sloping mountain trail—one filled with false summits, steep ascents, and unexpected stumbles. Thankfully, I've had good company helping me keep my footing.

To my son, Kellen Sansone—my first reader—thank you for your patience, honesty, and encouragement. Your thoughtful feedback pushed me past my own reluctance. And to my other son, Andrew Cooper-Sansone, I'm grateful for your active curiosity, inquiry, and belief in me.

To Maria, José, Donna, Hilary, and Marielle, whose life stories I am honored to share—I am deeply grateful for your generosity and courage. Your willingness, tenacity, and openness to spirit in the face of great adversity are testaments to its power to shape and guide our lives in our search for meaning and purpose.

To my editors, Luc Hatlestad and Angela Wiechmann, your skill, patience, and ability to organize my thoughts while keeping my voice intact. To my friend and reader, Alexis Miles, for your sensitive and skillful insight. To the editors and publishers at Collective Ink, thank you for your dedication, insight, and belief in this work. Your commitment to sharing transformative ideas and your thoughtful guidance has brought this book into the hands of the right reader.

I would not have been able to write this book without those who guided me deeper into spirit.

Cody Wiggs, for skillfully leading me into the unknown regions of psyche as the exceptional therapist you were—and, in spirit, undoubtedly still are. Stacia Blanc, for your generosity and down-to-earth way of helping me to connect to and trust my guides and the unseen as I faced old life challenges anew. Lazaros Bountour, for your healing shamanism and for helping me grasp what lies beyond. Victoria Garcia, who made all the difference in beginning this work. As a trusted advisor and compassionate medium, you conveyed the message that I had made a pre-life agreement to write this book. I am forever grateful to the teachers, staff, leadership, and students of the Quadrinity Process at the Hoffman Institute Foundation for showing me the beauty and freedom found in courageously transforming suffering into spiritual liberation. At pivotal moments, the right person can have a profound impact. Annabelle Nelson, I am deeply grateful for your gentle yet firm guidance at the Fielding Graduate Institute, which led me to embrace writing as a path to knowing and sharing what truly matters. To my brothers in life and spirit—Andrew Bunin, Andy Churgin, Burke Miller, Drew Horning, and Eric Schulz—whose two decades of connection, wisdom, and shared exploration have grounded and inspired me, blending strength with vulnerability, insight with action, and reflection with purpose. I was never the lone author of this book—just the one pushing the pen. Thank you to my guides. This book may have been on my to-do list before I came into this life, but I was never alone in bringing it to life. And finally, to my life partner, Maria Velasco—with absolute gratitude. If ever there are soul mates—I'm certain that we are. Your belief in me and in my mission to complete this book have been rare gifts. Above all is your unwavering commitment to living each day with compassion, authenticity, and awareness, guided by the loving longing of your soul.

Introduction

Have you ever, even for a fleeting moment, felt exhilarated, completely alive and present to yourself? Have you had a moment when you surrendered in awe to a mystical or spiritual experience, an ecstatic moment, however brief or extended of love, in meditation, in yoga, in prayer, or in solitude among trees, gazing at towering mountains, beneath a star-filled night sky, or upon vast open water—a moment when time seemed to stand still? A moment when surrendered and all aspects of you merged in harmony and joined in flow with something far bigger than you—a seamlessness between yourself and all living beings? You were filled with pure joy by something more real than anything in your everyday reality. And what followed was such a new way of seeing, with clarity and understanding, that it changed the trajectory of your life.

These are life-defining experiences of *Enlightenment*. According to global research studies by neurologist Andrew Newberg, M.D., Professor and Director of Research, Marcus Institute of Integrative Health at Thomas Jefferson University and Hospital. Newberg's work reports prolific measurable effects of spiritual experiences on the brain, finding that there's chain reactions of spiritual development starting with small 'e' enlightenments, that are brief and pave the way for the big 'E' ones intense and ecstatic. Big or small, these are glimmers into what your soul is longing for you to know and to become.

Deep within each one of us churns a seemingly irrepressible longing, that speaks a subtle often confounding language that emits an aching that we have carried since birth, powered by a higher intelligence. It is signaling us to dig within ourselves and release tremendous healing and creative powers embedded within us. Longing comes directly from our soul which wants us to transcend the old pain of suffering, to know and embrace our purpose, and to claim our share of universal peace. Our soul is longing for us to be loving of ourselves right now, just as we are, and to live inspired so that we manifest our true calling. However, most of us have been conditioned from childhood to ignore our longing, perceiving it only as an irritating pain caused by some persistent problem we need to fix. The good news is that, despite our best efforts to suppress it, our soul's longing never disappears. Longing is a wellspring of vitality, continually guiding us toward a more enlightened life where we are free to be our true selves. In truth, most of us, at some level, already know this.

There is substantial evidence of a growing global trend, particularly in the U.S., of people embracing spirituality and seeking to live a unique, inspiring purpose. This trend is particularly noticeable among younger generations, including Millennials and Gen Z, who are driving a shift away from traditional religious practices toward a more individualized and inclusive approach to spirituality. Research also shows that a significant number of Americans are becoming more spiritual over time. A recent Pew Research Center survey found that 41 percent of U.S. adults report becoming more spiritual throughout their lives, with only 13 percent saying they have become less so; and 83 percent of all U.S. adults believe people have a soul or spirit in addition to their physical body.

While traditional religious affiliation is declining, spirituality is on the rise. This shift is seen in the way people now consider spirituality, often describing it as a connection to something greater than themselves, such as nature or the universe. The growing inner quest among us leads to seeking a deeper, more inspiring purpose for being alive. What we are seeing is an unfurling of intuitive ways of knowing that every fiber of life—of nature, of humankind—is universally connected and fundamentally imbued by creative power and mystery, that we can directly access. That we are here to reveal and to bring to life our own inner mystery through the use of our minds, by the vibrations of our hearts, and through the medium of our bodies by whatever means that might take on for each of us. And there's more. By reaching deep within us we inevitably affect so much beyond ourselves: As we heal ourselves, and as others heal themselves, we heal the planet and contribute to the evolution of humankind.

Our most formidable obstacles to living and sharing our own creative power and mystery arise from the erosion of ancient forces—programmed limiting ways of thinking, feeling, acting, and believing about life, about one another, and about ourselves—that cling to us and rob us of our precious vitality. We all carry some version of them, some more, some less— robotic-like, reactive, habitual, self-destructive ways of coping with life. We learned them in childhood—most were etched into our psyches before we could know it, with edges now honed sharply by repetition. No matter how much they tried or how good our parents were, or how hard we tried, we've all, since day one, carried toxic shamed-based beliefs about ourselves that were never true in the first place.

In the following pages, you'll be encouraged to take a closer look at how you've unknowingly learned habits that were passed down to you and how it has become more than living with them, but rather how you've managed to live around or even in spite of them. We hold onto so many of the old ways as if our life depends upon them, because we think it does. We were sold shares, and bought into a fallacy, that we had to have those ways for no less than our survival. Living from them we've made costly sacrifices, avoided opportunities to accept love, or we gave away far too much of our precious energy, all of it to shield our hurting hearts and to prove our worth embarrassed by our imperfections. All of that has even wider repercussions.

Many of us unfortunately were raised to become spiritually bereft. Most of us were not taught to listen for ourselves at the level of Spirit, and much more, how to follow its signals. Instead, we were taught, mostly by omission and numbing, to ignore it. Yet there is a spiritual longing that persists: when our minds are calm it whispers to us, when least expecting its synchronicities delight us, asleep we dream of it, moments of enrapturing flow delight us; it also comes by alarming shocks that shake us.

The pages ahead will inform, encourage, and equip you with new skills, while also reinforcing ones you already have, to help you connect with your deeper spiritual being by letting go of the stubborn bindings of old habits. And, most importantly, they will deepen your connection to your soul so that you can enjoy its complexity and its richness, rekindling your true passion, and reawakening the inspiring truth of who you are and what you came to do in this lifetime. This may involve revisiting some of your pain, but viewing it as having a sacred purpose, as Paramahansa Yogananda suggested when he said, "Pain is a prod to remembrance."

The pages ahead offer an invitation for you to embark upon an inner pilgrimage to skillfully confront old fears, transcend their pain, and see through to their divine intentions. The first two chapters explore the instinctual and habitual levels of awareness that shape our human experience from birth. Chapters three through eight delve into intentional decision-making and the creative potential of imagination at the level of personality. Finally, chapters nine through fourteen offer immersive, self-reflective experiences designed to inspire higher, transformational awareness.

Through guided exercises you will have opportunities to uncover and overcome barriers that have been holding you back from your abundance of love and positivity. I'll also offer ways of revisioning yourself as a mystery to be explored—a creative, whole being who's every answer is reachable by pathways already within you.

The soul seeks change but the egoic logic-based mind likes to keep things as they are. So, to get around the ego's blocks

Introduction

some parts of this book are written in *soul language*. Soul language evokes deeper, more holistic ways of knowing for the mind, for the heart and for the body by—intuiting pure perception, releasing emotions, and sensing vibrations. For this I provide some guided exercises for opening you to your soul's flow directly from your subconscious to your everyday consciousness.

Along the way I'll also offer short takes from philosophy and from ancient ways of knowing that shed light on the nature of the soul. Stories of five people—people just like you and me—will show the enormous heart-opening possibilities of courageously turning into, not away from, their pain. Their verses will help you to reflect upon your own experiences and motivate you to appreciate your resiliency and to see the wisdom that you have gleaned from your own adverse experiences.

You will be continuously encouraged, through guided experiences, to come close to your true self, to meet yourself at the level of your soul, and to connect with your purpose.

Being engaged in continuous search, discovery, and refinement of one's purpose, or purposes as it might be, is essential to living a fulfilled life. Besides, to be engaged that way is powerfully influential to all the rest of humanity. To become our authentic selves causes a ripple effect on others to pursue theirs too. Lynne Twist, author and visionary, emphasizes in her book, *Living a Committed Life*, that a clear and compelling vision—what I often refer to as 'purpose'—is essential for transforming our lives and the world, that true vision will inspire us, pull us out of fear, and away from despair, will guide our actions, and give us the courage to believe beyond what we had imagined possible.

In my childhood trauma recovery, and continued personal development, I have benefitted from positive assumptions, and by ease of access to healing and education resources—psychotherapy, neurofeedback, meditation, martial arts, yoga, time in nature and travel (free to roam most anyplace, anytime), and the Hoffman Quadrinity Process (twice).

Writing this book has been heart-opening and mind-expanding. It began serendipitously at the onset of COVID when, sequestered at home, I began receiving, in slow drips, inspirations that I later understood as subtle messages coming from my soul, many of which I wrote down and now appear verbatim in especially the third part of the book. As you read the pages ahead, I hope that you'll feel similar to how I felt writing them: that you're embarking on a rewarding and fulfilling concentration on yourself, of ease and flow, of relief and of joy, of emotional expressiveness, and divine connection to your own authentic loving self.

Begin
It is time
you know it,
I know it
why delay?
Just this,
fear, shame, rage,
immobility, cluelessness,
condemnation,
self-destruction.

Dare not dance with these characters
not worthy of your god within.
See, know, welcome
them each into your house,
make peace.

Undress, remove masks, reveal facade,
deceptions learned far before, and now.
Enliven them to the mercifulness of

empathy,
compassion,
and love of you
cradled into
your true-nature,
a surrender-seeking-Self,
following its unseen freedom.

Chapter One

The Wound and the Lie

> *People tell us from the time we are born that the world is such and such and so and so, and naturally we have no choice but to accept that the world is the way people have been telling us it is.*
>
> *—Carlos Castaneda, Journey to Ixtlan*

Today's river of humanity was formed by the merging of diverse ancient societies that flowed throughout time and over vast distances. Fossil records tell us that our earliest human ancestors began in Africa more than 1.5 million years ago. Those who first utilized tools and weapons appeared on the scene around 150,000 years ago, while others capable of advanced communication via symbols came on about 70,000 years ago.

Noted paleoanthropologists Lee Berger and John Hawks, report that adaptation and survival of our remarkable species has been slow and gradual, organic, and complex. At the dawn of modern humankind, Africa already was rich in different traditions, reflecting myriad learnings accumulated and passed down over thousands of years. Along the evolutionary road, different hominid species crossbred and interlaced DNA. They also blended unique ways of forming societies, refining their roles and collective behaviors needed for survival—hunting and gathering food, dominating landscapes, fending off predators, protecting themselves and their societies from competitors, cooperating with others, child-rearing, and putting their dead to rest. They learned from outsiders, from their cousins, parents, and grandparents, and passed those ways on to their children—traditions that continue with us modern folks. Of course, in humankind's early millennia, when basic survival was the goal, there was little time or opportunity to tend to one's psychological, emotional, or spiritual paucity.

Wounded at Birth

At our own evolutionary sequel, long before any of us had any ability to realize it, each of us would become another part of a chain reaction drawing us away from ourselves and into an illusory state of separation treading in a pool of shame. Regardless of geography, culture, race, or gender, this would happen to each of us—devolving spellbound by a robust conditioning process that began at birth. Some psychologists refer to it as *the mother wound*: caused by a lack of attentiveness to the child's needs by their mother, which leads to insecure attachment. But there's more to it than that.

Before a child enters this world, they exist at-one with their mother's womb—a secure and comforting cocoon known as their only home. There is no distinction between the fetus' self and its safe place: they're merged. But then, in the conspicuous instant of birth, the spell is broken, and a baby is thrust us into a frenzied, foreign, and hostile environment, depriving them of the solace known only moments before.

In this new and foreign world, every experience will excite the infant's nascent brain. Syntax of newly forming neural circuitry absorbs oncoming foreign stimuli outside of, and within the baby's body. Though separate, an infant is virtually unable to discern itself from the world around it and from anybody else. Like sensory sponges, experience is sieved through eons of ingrained human survival instincts signaling the baby to stay alive. Sensations foreign in the womb—thirst and hunger, abrupt sounds, harsh lights, sudden movements—pierce their senses. There is no distinguishing whether these are passing blips or lethal threats. In the midst of it all how could an infant completely trust that it is safe? Author and spiritual guide, Nita Gage, suggests that it could not:

"Babies clearly do not trust that they will be fed; they scream when hungry. Survival seems to depend on a lack of trust and a ferocious determination to demand that our needs be met."

Suspended in states of utter dependency and reactivity, possessing no ability to move away from harm or toward safety, an infant is virtually helpless—and viscerally, knows it. At times it seemed the body was as if a house on fire, and the baby was trapped inside.

Soon, the infant child's brain's evolving cerebrum will enable greater awareness of its situation of separateness, helplessness, and complete dependence. Instinctively, the infant will learn to double down, reach out for and cling to those godlike powers—its caregivers—the sole source of its safety, nutrition, and comfort. To move beyond survival and to thrive, an infant needs a dependable bond, viscerally to know that they won't be abandoned. But, inevitably, even the firmest, most committed parent-child bonds will become rife with breaks many times over.

In the ideal perfect state parents serve as a child's source of protection, confidence, and warmth which many do, much of the time. Even so, the most well-intentioned parent, consciously or unconsciously, becomes a child's first source of threat. What can pose inevitable threats to a child's autonomy arise when parents assert their expectations for compliance—encouraging them to be a 'good baby'—and later, to conform to societal ideals by being obedient (getting along well with others) and productive (proving their worth) as a member of the family and society. The trade-off for the child's obeyance is the parents' protection, sustenance, and warmth. At the end of the day, a child sees in the eyes, senses by the tone of voice, and discerns by the body language the effects of stress and strain that everyday life puts upon their parents. A child instinctively knows and stays attuned for the sake of their own survival, that they mustn't add to their parents' burdens. To ensure their own survival and sense of belonging, they must behave and be good. This means skillfully anticipating their moods, quirks, likes and dislikes, placing the child's attention squarely on the adult.

Out of our own personal quests for survival and belonging we each ingeniously learned to be, act, feel, gesture, and speak in line with our caregivers, just as our caregivers had to do with their caregivers. Nobody had any other conceivable choice but to adapt to those holding the power—internalize their ways, mimic their emotional expressions, and adopt (or rebel against) their beliefs—or we would have all perished a long time ago.

More often than not, many children are reflexively sustaining a delicate balance between concealing their own inner pressures and not overwhelming their parents. Most of the time, strategies of adapting and complying—being good and behaving as their parents wish—works to the child's advantage, survival-wise. A child's outburst risks their parent's wrath, or worse, their disappearance. But, at another level, a child is undergoing lifelong conditioning of ignoring their own true self.

Inheriting Lovelessness

The purest nature of a young child is innocence. From ages two to four, children are in the early stages of forming their personal identity: understanding that there is a difference between one's *me* and another's *you*. It's a tough dilemma, with such ambiguity challenging for a child to navigate. As with all developmental challenges a child must face, choices are rarely clear cut and outcomes are rarely absolute. From the outside looking in, what appears as a stable homelife a child might actually be experiencing aloneness, disorientation, and fear. Even so, most children are resilient, and their survival instinct runs deep. Despite occasional temper tantrums in protest, a three-year-old inherently knows that as they must move in the direction of becoming their own unique self they must also continue adapting and yielding to their all-powerful caregivers as their first priority. It's a delicate balancing act that requires great finesse for the child to fit itself into the mold impressed upon them: if the child does not fit into the mold, then it must be the child who is wrong, not the mold.

Most children become masterful at surviving by habituating. By the time a child reaches middle childhood, its rapidly expanding cerebral cortex will devise more complicated and sophisticated ways of adapting to many new, untried realities. Eventually survival would depend on the ability to predict and control and to react fittingly: cataloguing the especially useful strategies. Along the way they'd gather meaning from their experiences to be stored away in the safe of their expanding visceral memory.

At the same time, the child's caregivers would be facing their own dilemmas, tough times, and ripening inner conflicts. It's safe to say that most parents aspire to love their children fully and freely and vow to do their best for them; at the same time, they're still seeking refuge from painful experiences from their own past, as it might be they too were trapped inside their own burning house. Because they, too, had learned the same process of survival—that their parents' love and care came with conditions, some great, some less, some explicit, some implicit. In the end approval, care, and protection were provided in exchange for complying and abiding. It was an unspoken solid pact, a time hewed fully replicable blueprint. Without knowing how to truly love themselves, a parent cannot unconditionally love their child. By omission they'd pass along a lineage of lovelessness without intending to. It's an unavoidable highwire act that not one of us, parent or child, balances perfectly. And, by the time we reach middle childhood most of it is hard wired within us.

As a child grows into a young adult—traversing new terrain and negotiating relationships with other kinds of people outside the family—they'll try to navigate those using the same map charted at home. If raised in a well-balanced family many of those ways will work out well enough. Of course, a young adult can learn and can change: they'll find new, authentic ways of being with people that support their emerging new self. But what's bound to be troublesome is playing out old stubborn scripts of the left-over unhealed, self-defeating, unconscious habits, and experiencing frustration in expecting different results when hitting up against the same exhausting outcomes. We were fooled into believing that true inner love was sourced from outside of us and is not completed by turning inward to reap abundant loving guidance from our own true Self.

Amidst all this, there is still within the person their essence, untouched by all of the personality's learned painful behaviors and the shame they carry which might only be muffled, not made lesser. There, too, is the soul of the person calling to connect and find a new way forward. These powerful forces are outside typical levels of awareness. Learning to close the distance between obliviousness and becoming one with one's essence is life's most profound quest. And yet, we have no choice but to immerse ourselves in our shame so that we can find our way out of the gripping state of self-alienation. Every human being experiences this primal struggle.

Every person, in varying depths, has been led into an unavoidable alternate reality that began with a misconstrued belief that they are undeserving of absolute love simply "because." Everyone has a good heart, fully capable of loving; the only difference is how deeply it's buried. Some of us have to dig deeper than others. But it is there for each of us to uncover. Even so, the question looms large: Why?

From birth onwards we each became entwined by that absurdly, perfectly designed phenomenon of disconnecting us from our innermost being, destined to repeat with every baby born. Why does it happen? Do we live only to survive? Or might the phenomenon serve our evolution beyond mere survival?

Visionary Bob Hoffman dubbed the phenomenon, *negative love syndrome*—a separation of oneself from one's essence that begins at birth. To overcome its harmful effects, Hoffman developed the Hoffman Quadrinity Process, where participants become aware of the uniqueness of their own negative love condition, resolve to forgive their caregivers and themselves, and move beyond the residue of habitual ways, open their selves to their own spiritual essence to align with their authenticity. Similarly, in her book *There's Nothing Wrong with You*, author Cheri Huber offers a Buddhist perspective when she describes the same phenomenon and traces it to the absolute origin of self-hate that we all experience to varying degrees. bell hooks, in her discussions about love and familial relationships, also explores how dysfunctional family dynamics can perpetuate cycles of emotional absence into stubborn generational trauma and deny persons of their capacity to regard themselves in loving terms and do the same with others.

Spiritual counselor, energy worker, and author Pamela Kribbe, who over the course of several years has collected and published inspired messages channeled from an incarnate being, *Jeshua* (the Aramaic name for Jesus), refers to this uncanny design as *inherited lovelessness*. She presents it in spiritual terms and traces it to deep ancestral patterns, including emotional wounding by abandonment, abuse, and neglect. These inherited emotional wounds are often rooted in feelings of living bereft of unconditional love lost in existential separation and leading one away from their divine essence.

As we will explore in the pages ahead, the closer we look the clearer we can see that by its painful tension and existential limitations, inherited lovelessness imposes on our lives, and upon our souls hereafter, a choice remains for us: To become truly free, we must choose to overcome our condition of dependency, act, and embrace our own heart-based consciousness. Kribbe channels such a message from Jeshua:

> *In the moment of your cosmic birth, the moment that desolation and pain enveloped you, you started to feel tiny and*

insignificant. From that moment on, you started to look for something that could save you—a power or force outside of you, a god, a leader, a partner, a child ... the essential safety you are longing for is not to be found in anything outside of you, whether it's a parent, a lover or a god ... There is nothing outside you that can bring you into the heart of your own power, your own wholeness. You are it; you are the one and you have always been the one!

Our sense of incompleteness was never a flaw of ours; it is an invitation from our soul beckoning us to live beyond survival and to reconnect with our absolute innate source of truth and wholeness. Arriving at this realization—that the way to our fulfillment has been within us all along—is the beginning of a transformative journey to living truth, beauty, and peace within. The self-limiting habits of inherited lovelessness were learned unconsciously and, they can be unlearned consciously. It requires us to choose to move forward in life in a new and authentic way by freeing ourselves of the illusion that our parents were ever to be our ultimate source of love and approval and finding ultimate acceptance and regard by the god of love that has been dwelling, waiting, and calling from within us.

***

The following is an invitation for you to connect with your inner child, acknowledge your striving to survive, and offer yourself the compassion you deserved back then.

Make yourself comfortable and take a few deep breaths. Bring to mind an image of yourself as a child of any age, trusting that the right one will come to you. Turn to and look with compassion into the eyes of this innocent child knowing that their memory is still present within you.

Allow your imagination to help you see through the eyes of this child. Bring to mind a scene of a particular event that was difficult for them. What was happening? What were they feeling? What do you know about their pain and where it came from?

You might feel the hurt still now within your body today. What are you feeling? Where do you feel it? What needs to be released? What within you needs healing?

Move in closer to your child. When did your hurt originate? How did it happen? Perhaps you were deceived, let down, brushed aside, frightened, abandoned, or ignored? Simply being with your hurt is a generous way of caring for yourself. Be present to your innocent child within and meet them with love.

Open yourself to your own compassion. Receive your own tenderness. Call forth your expansive, sympathetic heart and tell yourself that you deeply love who you are today and as you were as a child back then. Consider softly saying aloud these words to yourself: *I deeply love you. No matter how, in the past, I might have misunderstood, ignored, neglected, or abandoned you—I do love you. There is nothing that can ever make me want to distance myself from you ever again. I am sorry for how I ignored you, numbed you, or made you feel less than anything other than the extraordinary child that you were. I honor you; you have always been perfect. I am grateful for your resiliency, creativity, curiosity, wisdom, playfulness, and tenderness. I am always here for you. We are together now as one, as we will be for this moment now and forever.*

Take a deep breath and let out a sigh of relief as you settle into the compassionate space within yourself, a space you've made even more expansive. This vitality, born from your own love, is here to bring you healing. By opening yourself to your past wounds, you are fulfilling one of your soul's deepest intentions—to grow in love. Welcome this bond of renewal that your soul is yearning to create.

Longing

As you go about your days, practice listening for the unique whisper of your soul. You might simply invite it in, in ways and at times that feel right for you. Even if you may be grappling with disbelief, know that your soul is tenderly offering you a safe path to healing. Your soul is never adversarial, never guilting or withholding, and it holds the power to nurture you fully. It longs for you to join with it through the power of love. Open yourself to it and receive.

Chapter Two
Irony of Shame

Shame is the wish to diminish ourselves—or as author and expert on the effects of shame, Joseph Burgo, puts it: "Shame arouses a wish to become invisible." John Bradshaw, whose books on shame have informed professionals and non-professionals alike for decades, sheds light on its origins and effects. He argues that each of us undergoes a systematic and unavoidable immersion into toxic shame risking profound effects: the absence of self-love, the presence of self-loathing, lethargy, erosion of self-esteem, the breakdown of families as safe and secure systems, and an ongoing inability to form lasting, intimate relationships throughout life. Toxic shame—convincing us that we are inherently unlovable—can deeply harm our sense of self and how we perceive our worth. Early on, we internalized this belief while striving for love and acceptance, often through pleasing others or performing for approval, all the while abandoning our true selves. Naturally, we sought to escape this inner turmoil, but it came with profound risks.

Early attempts, as children, to challenge the myth of being inherently unlovable—if we even knew how—felt like an even greater threat to our survival. Exposing this belief risked abandonment, making it safer to remain aligned with and protected by our caregivers. In this desperate bid for safety, we kept our true selves hidden and stayed blind to our innate lovability. This seemingly cruel, inescapable conundrum left us trapped in a scarcity of self-love, disconnected from our inherent magnificence, and unaware of our brilliance.

In our innocence, we mistakenly learned to try to find wholeness outside of ourselves, though in reality it could only be found within. As we grew older, we continued to search outward, hoping to soothe the deep, often overwhelming pain of separation. This pain left us feeling exhausted, unfulfilled, and disconnected from our true purpose. In doing so, we inadvertently created an existential void.

In our quest to fill our vacancy, we sought refuge in all sorts of distractions—activities, possessions, and identities. We believed that accomplishments, work, money, titles, and status could finally make us feel whole, and prove that we were lovable. We tried to carve out a place of recognition in the world by embodying certain roles and ways of proving them by being smart, kind, loud, quiet, giving, clever, important, attractive, knowledgeable, influential, selfless people person, or ready problem solver. Surely, we thought, these would bring us the peace we longed for. Yet often there lingers a subtle, persistent feeling of something unfinished. A lull of emptiness, a flatness, as if something is just beyond our reach, tiring by the chase. None of this is ill-intended: It's just misguided.

From infancy we were conditioned to believe that other people of power were the sole and leading source of the sense of acceptance and love we so desperately craved. Very few of us were guided to know otherwise. Most of our closest life teachers—our parents, caregivers—never knew the truth, either. So logically, we all kept on looking outward and coming up short: what we needed to find was unseeable, invisible, unknowable by the logical mind that had been conditioned to believe in this lie of inherited lovelessness and to see its shaming way. Naturally we all were living in murky waters. But now, as adults, we can clearly see the unintended effects of our past conditioning. We can choose a new life connected with the ever-present, generous lover and unfailing guide within us—our soul. It has been waiting patiently, ready to lead us toward the fulfillment and peace we've been seeking all our lives.

We see that when left unchecked, shame has a way of creeping through the shadows of our minds, distorting and corrupting our thoughts. It weaves a web of lies about who we are and the purpose of our existence. This is why healing the wound of shame as our first sacred priority plays a pivotal role in our journey toward self-love, our authenticity, and our spiritual evolution.

Shame's Paradox

Consider the irony that shame actually serves a profound and sacred end: that there's more to it than the agony it initiates. That our wounding by shame is not merely accidental but is purposeful and catalytic. That, despite its complex manifestations, shame presents a simple point of contrast. Like grit in the oyster, shame festers the right measure of irritation for us to want to awaken to the perfection of our spirit and commit ourselves to the path of our soul: shame's discomfort and disruption beckons us to traverse an unknown journey in hopes of finding what most inspires and fulfills us.

That we have shame is a human paradox: we, inherently lovable, spiritual beings, must release its bondage to grasp that we are indeed loveable. Put another way, shame is like a keyhole through which we must pass to truly be at peace.

We are born into a world of conflicting interdependent forces just as those of the natural world's ebbing and flowing of the oceans' tides, the changing of the seasons, a predator's pursuit and a prey's alert, by the delicacy of flowers and the ferocity of hurricanes. Life abounds with paradoxes—calling upon all creatures each day to balance conflicting forces acting upon and within them: masculinity and femininity; defense and vulnerability; stability and change; force and gentleness; working and resting; satiation and hunger; living and dying. We are of the force's yin and yang: striving for harmony and equilibrium among disequilibrium; seeking order amid chaos;

finding life within death. We are together with our Earth endlessly creating and renewing our existence.

Within the order there is always risk. As in a well-acted drama—the drama of our lives, actually—shame plays a profoundly influential role: it is the internal antagonist creating conflict by fueling the hero's (our) self-doubt, isolation, and fear of vulnerability. The forces of shame can hinder the hero's decision-making, bristle confidence, impair relationships, and drive the hero into moral compromise. Shame may isolate the hero, prevent them opening up to help, instilling self-doubt, and dampening their power. Ultimately, though, it is meant to serve as a catalyst for evolutionary growth. As an alchemist confronting shame, the hero surmounts risk, achieves redemption, and becomes wiser by it all, turning inner turmoil into a transformative experience then once and for all, reuniting with the soul.

Whenever we choose to step into our core power, we become immersed in dimensions of ourselves that we never knew existed we become heroes of our soul. In the pages ahead we will hear from five people who bravely navigated intense life challenges and connected to the power of their soul and Spirit.

Stepping onto the path is often the most difficult part.

Whisper from Within

If we are to escape the web of shame, disentangle ourselves from all residues of a belief in worthlessness and dependency, and ascend to heart-based consciousness, we must seek, tune into, and listen closely for the quiet voice of the soul within. Tapping in is an art.

There is an ever-present whisper, endlessly beckoning us inward, reminding us that the answers we seek flow through channels within. Our longing, which we have sorely misunderstood, avoided, or tried to fix, is not a flaw but an invitation waiting to be recognized and embraced through the light of a new, heart-centered consciousness. This inner yearning, unique to each of us—because it comes from our soul—seeks to guide us toward ultimate fulfillment, revealing that the path begins with recognizing and embracing our own divine nature. By our longing our soul is asking us to listen closely and to follow its tireless yearning for freedom from the confines of lovelessness that we've inherited and might continue perpetuating.

Our longing is a deep desire to remember that we are beings made of love. True joy arises in accepting this truth without the need to prove our worthiness—for love naturally seeks love. The subtle art of listening for the quiet voice of our longing defines the true art of our lives: reaching absolute love of ourselves.

This is our longed-for destiny.

Embracing our longing requires courage to step away from what we think has been keeping us safe. The ego, whose core function is keeping us secure, safe, and stable has a toolbox full of powerful psychological techniques that have been evolving over the course of human evolution that can, and often do, predominate our sense of reality. So much so that the louder voice of the ego muffles the subtler calling of our soul. Beneath baseless chatter fed by self-hatred, shame, and doubt, ego creates an alternate reality that is aimed at numbing us. Still, there vying for our attention stays the gentle persistent whisper of our soul's longing for a fulfilling way of being. It wants us to find and occupy our space of soul where there is nothing we must prove or do: We must simply know that we are already *It* and *It* is seeking us, to be with us. As Ralph Waldo Emerson observed:

> When I watched that flowing river, which, out of regions I see not, pours for a season its streams into me, I see that I am a pensioner; not a cause but a surprised spectator of the ethereal water; that I desire and look up and put myself in the attitude of reception, but from some alien energy the visions come.

Envision yourself alone atop the peak of a great mountain. It's early summer, the air is warming. You are safely standing, able to see clearly in all directions and forever: expansive vistas of sloping rises, peaks, slopes, and valleys, brimming fresh streams flowing beneath azure skies. As the ice and snow of winter is thawing and becoming fluid, flowing, their runoff seeps into your mountain's many crevasses, descends into narrow tributaries, cascades into tiny feeder creeks, rushes into rapid freestone streams, all of it making its way downstream to empty into a broad river carrying all of its waters across landscapes to be empties at a delta of an ocean's gulf. As you watch, the water of your river mingles with the water of others contributing to the seamless interconnection of Earth's five great ocean basins forming a single global sea each one a living, unfolding mystery fertile with seeds of love and imbued with pull-out-all-stops intention to becoming spectacularly in love with ourself.

Like particles of ice and snow melting upon rays of the Sun's heat, we each will complete our own travels on this temporary home of Earth, where it becomes our fate before the death of many lives, to meet countless passages and hewn our soul's perfection. Upon reaching our completion we will rejoin the Great ending our cycles of evaporating, falling, and flowing. Each passage we make is indeed different and unique, and so each illuminates the truth of our unique soul and the myriad contributions that its perfection has made to the one great ocean.

Although there's often an overriding tendency pushing us to forget this inherent truth, the reliable tugging of longing, like a great internal magnet, keeps drawing us to its promise of finding true nature. It's what our own child so desperately longed for at the beginning.

Chapter Three

Pilgrimage of Longing

Longing arrives on the waves of whispers. Stirring from the depth of our void within—immersive, unwavering—its messages are sent by the sacred language of the soul to guide us back to the cosmic truth where we, as sparks of the universal whole, remain in a terminal state of waiting. We are waiting and seeking to grasp the purpose of our existence, to awaken to our divine essence within.

The intensity of the challenge to our awakening depends on how firmly we've concealed the truth of who we are. Despite our innate longing for love and acceptance, we've been taught to mask our vulnerabilities: bury wounds of lovelessness under layers of conditioning. Our hurts hidden away stand as barriers between us and our authentic selves, disconnecting from the very source of healing we crave. Yet, beneath those layers, the truth of our being still whispers, patiently waiting for us to unearth, reconnect, and rediscover its transformative power of self-love. The journey back to truth begins when we dare to reveal what we've hidden for so long.

Only by unearthing can we begin the discovery of wholeness. To paraphrase the 12th century mystic Rumi: It's as if we've been sitting on a pot of gold and have been too clueless to dig. Especially ironic is knowing that the soul's clues to dig have been vying for our attention our entire lives. Typically, they come at first subtly—by our dreams at night; by day-to-day synchronicities; and, by our intuition. Rarely do they outright rap us on the head. However, if unanswered for too long, or if time is running short and circumstances dire, the soul might intensify its messaging.

Longing is the summoning of a lifelong pilgrimage into the heart of who each of us truly is: the evolutionary thrust bent on exposing a best kept secret. But the soul abhors waste and will conceal until we're sufficiently ready for its wonders. Though from infancy onwards every soul longs for immersion into unity with the original source, rarely do we recognize its calling by usual ways of logical mind. That's the bulk of the problem.

Longing unmet might overwhelm the mind by summoning bravery to venture into the innerscape and explore what might, at the ordinary level of rational consciousness, appear as an unsolvable machination charged with enormous discomfort. The mind does battle: it reacts with skepticism, creative resistance, and abandonment of the self. But human beings have been endowed with the strength of curiosity for a far greater purpose than mere survival. Curiosity opens us to the strength of our innate need for exploration. Intrinsically we want to know—our soul wants us to know. So, it sends us non-ordinary clues to guide us to, through, and beyond confusion, most of the time though not instantaneously, as we might hope for, but assuredly.

Our soul's language is often cryptic, obscure, and at times illogical or absurd, we might not understand it or we might overlook it altogether. The soul, our evolutionary ally, reaches out, hoping to teach us how to recognize and heed its subtle call—guiding us through the riddle of taming the ego's commanding presence. Its passage is made through the inner door. The key to opening is our willingness and courage to sustain vulnerability—emotionally, and rationally too. We are obliged to embrace not knowing. To stand in vulnerability is a courageous act. It drives the rational mind wild with resistance. Vulnerability runs upstream in the current of survival. Only by that unique state—vulnerability borne of innocence and exposure—can we bloom open-hearted, curious, receptive to immense transformative power coming to us on the waves of the soul's whispers. We are obliged to keep aware and ready: no small task, that. And by no fault of our own there is much to overcome.

We are here with one over-arching purpose—to make peace with whatever holds us from knowing our blissful natural state. By clearing and committing to the path of our soul, we can transcend the victimhood of our childhood as active creators of our lives—empowered beings fully integrated with the essence of Spirit. The perplexed person of yesterday becomes today an empowered whole being of presence: imbued with the essence of Spirit, a living, breathing entity thriving in pursuit of its unique sacred purpose. We need not search for it far and away. Who we are, and who we are meant to become, has been seeded within us, unfolding through an evolutionary process that calls us to consciously engage with the extraordinary essence of our higher being—a tireless, transformative journey, weaving us ever closer to our true nature. In time, we all will align with this sacred process. And as we commit to doing so, we realize boundless possibilities—harmonizing with the uniqueness of others, contributing to the vast flow of creation, and thriving in the oneness that connects all beings. We are participating and contributing to what Ralph Waldo Emerson referred to as, "that Oversoul within which everyone's particular being is contained is made one with all other." We each are here to know and to live wholeheartedly this ultimate truth. Though, to get there we must first overcome the old limitations we've been shaped to believe.

At each of our own births a powerful spark of pure consciousness splintered into us from the Great Source of All. It's our life force, our *prana*, nested in a perpetual state of absolute love longing to return us home. Emerson reflected on this great symbiosis, this absolute quest for spiritual enlightenment, in describing the Oversoul:

> ...*the soul of the whole; the wise silence; the universal beauty, to which every part and particle is equally related, the eternal*

ONE ... *We see the world piece by piece, as the sun, the moon, the animal, the tree; but the whole, of which these are shining parts, is the soul.*

From the moment we are born, we are steered off course—away from revering our true Self and toward seeking approval and validation from others. Ironically, this misguided path takes root and grows, nourished by our need to experience perfect love. Instinctively, we hope to find this love reflected back to us by our caregivers. Yet, inevitably, they'd fail to meet such an impossible expectation. After enduring the pain of collapse, and knowing no better, we would righteously blame, holding our caregivers accountable for their perceived failures, to varying degrees. This cycle persists until the wound of inherited lovelessness is healed within us. Failing to heal ourselves poses a profound risk: the wounded child may grow into an adult trapped in the role of victim—blaming their parents, circumstances, partners, God, or even life itself. Stuck in this illusion of powerlessness, they remain disconnected from the truth of who they truly are, leaking power, and naïve about who they truly are. And so, it will go, as author Alain de Botton wrote: ". . . until the day we end our quixotic searches and reach a semblance of mature detachment, realizing that the only release from our longing may be to stop demanding a perfect love," and finally turning inward to what we had thought to be fallow soil, finding our own ardent being, then sowing, tending, and reaping boundless divine love awaiting us.

The Void

Within the self lies a magnificent void—a vast, innermost space that feels foreign to most. It is a reservoir of childlike purity and innocence; it is rich with raw emotion and essential memory from current and past lives. The void is a sacred place, a realm of the soul's wisdom, but over time we've learned to elude it—an instinctive effort to deflect the beliefs that it is dangerous. Yet, to confront and transcend these burdens, we humans possess a remarkable superpower.

Emotions are the language of the soul. Our emotions are our compass for homing in and guiding us to truth. Whether in response to a present moment or a remnant of the past each one carries an indelible felt sense meant to render us present to ourselves and land us in our hearts. Emotions come in immeasurable variety and complexity, in every shade, sensation, and intensity. We welcome feelings of awe, delight, enchantment, freedom, happiness, invigoration, radiance, renewal, vibrancy. And though we have to learn how, we can also learn to welcome those that make us feel uncomfortable — panic, desperation, angst, bewilderment, anger, loneliness, helplessness, horror, trepidation, worry, insecurity, hatred, fear. Regardless, each one of them, alone or in combination as mishmashes of opposites, are messages from the soul for leading us on adventuresome pathways to love, light, and wisdom.

***

Following is a gentle, guided experience designed to help you connect compassionately with the child of your memory.

To rejoin the path of the soul a courageous choice has to be made: to venture into the depths of inner abyss and meet the shame wound of inherited lovelessness head-on with the power of compassion. To try this in a manner that's brief, I invite you to recall a time of innocence in your life, as far back as you can remember. Imagine the child, as you were back then, at whatever age you imagine them to be. (*Allow yourself time enough to see an image, or to feel the presence of, or to hear the breathing of yourself as a very young child.*) Then, invite your child to come close to you. As they do, you provide them with a quiet and safe place to rest, to simply be together with you for a moment. Take a few breaths together as you become more comfortable with each other.

Look into their eyes. What do you notice about this child of you? This child has been with you your entire life. At many levels you know them well. In this moment, notice their hands, their hair, legs, and feet. Listen for any sounds they might be making. Be curious about the feelings of this little one. What sense do you have about this child? How does it feel to be with them? Call this child to come near enough so that you can hear them whisper to you. Ask them whatever you'd like to know about them. It might be questions like: What age are you? What are you feeling at this moment? What do you need? Listen closely and wait patiently. What are they experiencing? Allow yourself enough time to closely listen with your ears, to see them clearly with your eyes, and to feel their presence. How does it feel to be with this little one?

Notice if you're experiencing any indifference. Notice if you might want to ignore or push this child away out of your own discomfort, out of shame or disdain for who this child was. Often, we blame our child inside, in the same way that our child learned to blame themselves. Are you doing that now? If you are, simply notice this. Then open yourself to feeling compassion for this child. Take a deep long breath. With open arms, reach out and embrace your child, your own younger self. You know and appreciate, better than anyone, the gift of their innocence, their curiosity, the beauty of their being. Take a moment now to be with that.

As you deepen your connection with your inner child, notice how your heart softens and becomes more open, welcoming them fully. What is one or two qualities about them that you truly admire? Perhaps it's their joy, curiosity, playfulness, cleverness, or vibrant energy. Allow yourself to see their innocence clearly and feel your heart expanding with warmth and love as you honor these. You might know and feel this child's pain of not being seen or perhaps not fully appreciated for who they were. Please take a moment to be with whatever comes to you as you are patiently breathing. By your open heart you understand them and are seeking to understand them more.

Before ending this time together with your child for now, consider making a commitment to your child to check in on them from time to time. Remember, this child is an essential part of who you are today and is always available to share insights and feelings from your past. They are available to inform you about your present self whenever you need it. Your child is ready to receive your love and attention. They are ready to become free of old beliefs and ways of the past. They wait to enjoy the rest of the time you have together exploring, learning, changing, and growing. For now, send your child off to a safe place within you.

Grace's House
Knowing the Self is
drinking from Wisdom's fountain.
Longing for Soul is
living in the house of Grace.

Chapter Four
Soul Healing

At the Starland

Over the din of a late-night TV show, the motel switchboard phone rang: a few quick questions and answers. Tension swelled. Hesitancy. A handful of slow minutes dragged by. Dreading the worst, I left the office and made my way to one of the rooms at the Starland Motel. There, in the middle, stood an imposing White man, loosely holding a large handgun at his side, eyes cast detached on a slender young Black man, who lay unconscious, on a bed writhing in obvious pain. I had just turned fifteen and had no idea what to do.

For a week in the summer of 1973—the year of the U.S. Supreme Court's landmark decision, 'Roe v. Wade' protecting a woman's constitutional right to privacy—I was in Bay City, a small town in south Texas. I was visiting a childhood friend, Will, who had recently moved to Ft. Worth, and former coach from my Catholic parochial school in South St. Louis, "Big Jack."

Born in rural Missouri, raised in poverty, and abandoned by his birth father, Jack would never marry or have children. Many of us young boys, ages ten to early teens, were fascinated by him, we came to idolize him for his gripping stories of past brutal boxing matches and violent street fights (he had the scars to prove them). Jack vented pent-up rage through racist and homophobic theories, slurs, and rantings (though never in the presence of our parents). He had a fascination with guns (which he also kept from our parents). He indulged our appetites for junk food, sports equipment, bowling, smoking, cussing, fighting, and hard-core pornography. We kids were getting the rare gift of an adult's undivided time and attention, and access to all other sorts of 'privileges' far beyond our developmental capacity to manage them.

Our parents had no idea. Jack had manipulated the trust of my family, of other families, and our school administrators: he volunteered to coach athletics, which they eagerly accepted. He would leave St. Louis after inheriting the Starland.

The Starland was a 1930s motor court motel, low-slung and modest, blending into the flat land along the two-lane road to Bay City. Its rooms set in a simple horseshoe, opened toward a glassed-in office at one end. It was still operating, though long past its prime. The air on that July night, though the sun had set hours before, was especially thick with heat: clamoring katydid and cricket calls filled the airwaves like radio static. Jack, Will, and I, were in the office with the TV on, where the odor of that morning's burnt coffee lingered with the stink of another one of Jack's days-old cigars.

Will and I grew increasingly uneasy as Jack grew more and more agitated: pacing, glancing, cursing under his breath. He was keyed-in on one room just outside the office. He rang it from the switchboard a few times, and each time he did, they hung up on him. More cussing, grumblings, muttering racist, and homophobic slurs. Seething, Jack had reached a pitch. Slipping on a sport coat he tucked a forty-five-caliber pistol into the front of his belt and said that he was, "Going to check on those two."

I was a small White kid, hundreds of miles from home watching from inside, powerless, and helpless, as Jack stalked outside.

The office air conditioner hummed, and the TV blared. Holding our breath. Two of us, teenagers, stood still staring out of the window at the room vexed, helpless. Under the faded yellow glow of the sodium light, we saw Jack pound his fist on the door of the room. A few seconds passed, the door flung open as a young, blond, White man, clenching a towel around his waist, burst out, glancing over his shoulder before disappearing from view behind the motel. A few moments passed and the office phone rang. Will answered, listened, and then turned to me,

"Jack wants to know, do you know first aid?"

I had taken a class.

"He wants us to go over there. You go, and I'll stay and watch the switchboard."

Just as quick, I said,

"No, we both go!"

The distance to the room was short but it took a while to get there. I was petrified. Will waited outside the room, and I walked inside. Jack was standing in the middle, holding the gun at his side with a nonplussed look on his face. There wasn't any blood. A young Black man lay on the bed, unclothed, covered down from the waist by a bed sheet. He appeared unconscious, his entire body was convulsing, shaking uncontrollably, at times almost leaving the bed. The man's breathing was shallow and rapid. Groaning in obvious pain, he was clenching a towel in his teeth. Stunned, I stood and stared for a moment, clueless. Jack deadpanned,

"He said he was an epileptic and was going to have a seizure. He asked for the towel and went out."

Apparently to Jack, this was an inconvenience, at most a curiosity.

I had never witnessed what's now referred to by medical experts as a tonic-clonic seizure. I've since learned that if one lasts for more than five minutes, it is considered a medical emergency risking permanent brain damage, or death.

At once, I felt a shift within. And I barked: "Jack, put away the damn gun and call an ambulance!"

He and Will retreated to the office. I stayed there alone, in the room, with the man.

The little bit I knew about such a violent seizure was that a person risks breaking their teeth from intense clenching and that their throat might swell and drastically impede their breathing.

I climbed onto the bed straddling the man at his waist and steadying his shoulders. Lowering my right cheek to his right ear I'd whisper to him:

"You're going to be okay."

I wiped his face, his eyes, and his nose with the towel. His whole body was trembling—light shudders giving way to sudden, forceful convulsions, then settling for a few seconds into stillness. I continued whispering to him. Some time passed: the man and I connected this way. I was hoping that the moments of calm would last. Finally, they became longer. Eventually, stillness. Then, quiet. His breathing calmed and steadied. I felt a wave of relief. On this hot Texas night, it seemed he was going to be okay.

The door flung open, flashing red lights blazed the room like wildfire. Two White Matagorda County deputies, their two-way radios blaring, stepped in and took a furtive look around. Jack followed them. I was outraged: Jack, where's the ambulance?" He'd called the police, he deadpanned.

The man on the bed pitched back into violent convulsions. I was angry and demoralized. Eventually, an ambulance would arrive, and I'd be relieved. I was in over my head. Later, Will and I slipped away under the pale glow of a crescent moon, and got high.

And that was that. Will, Jack, and I said nothing more about it. In a few days, I'd return home marking the last time I would see or speak to Jack.

Just as one might stare at a familiar landscape without truly seeing it, it was only much later in my life that I came to understand the full gravity of that night upon who I was then and would become. I've wondered from where my courage, compassion, and presence of mind had come. I've wondered about the two young men in the room—particularly about the one who couldn't run away and hide, and who, if alive today, would probably be about seventy-five years old. That night he had been threatened, maltreated, and accosted for simply wanting to be with another peacefully in privacy. I've also wondered if he remembers that night—and, how it might have shaped him. Was it, perhaps, a lesson his soul had chosen to endure? Regardless, I respected him. At some level, at his soul's perhaps, he withstood an extreme situation with dignity. I also felt a kinship with him for reasons that would eventually become clear.

Compassion stems from the seeds of our inborn capacity for empathy—of awareness, sincerity, and willingness to conjure within oneself a felt sense of another person's emotions. Research shows that empathy generally begins developing as early as age two, amid a child's budding self-awareness. Compassion comes later on in life and goes a step further than empathy—it's when we actively respond to another person's suffering with warmth and actions of care. Compassion also differs from sympathy which is feeling concern and sorrow for another experiencing pain and hoping that their pain will be alleviated. This sense of suffering with another is possible even if we haven't experienced the same pain, or degree of it, in ourselves.

I had experienced compassion in an existential way by the stark contrast between two kinds of men: Jack's bruising callousness and the man's quiet dignity. With courage and poise in the face of an impending crisis, vulnerable in myriad ways, the man had asserted a simple yet profound request for self-care. I've often contemplated what had compelled my spur of the moment choice to act as I did. Perhaps his act of self-compassion and self-regard had inspired me to experience compassion and respect toward him. It might also be that in that instant I had perceived in him my own vulnerability, that until then, I had not been sufficiently aware. Not necessarily in a cosmic sense, although I believe that's possible too, but by witnessing his suffering I had grasped my own.

Con Men

The most insidious of child sex abuse offenders are the groomers who systematically prey on children and their families who grant them their trust. They're lowly con men (88% are male); who systematically entrap the psyche of children they target. Groomers (99% of all abusers) manipulate, isolate, threaten, and bribe a child into a waterproof pact of secrecy through suggestions like, "Let's just keep this between us." Or, "I'm doing this for you."

In the lingering fog of secrecy a child is mired in guilt and shame. Children are ego-centered, not out of grandiosity, but for the sake of surviving. So, mired in the secret they can be made to feel that they're responsible for it. The secrecy is isolating and constraining. A child's heart is frozen by fear. They're emotionally scarred, left with very little capacity to form trust with anyone: especially distrusting of themselves. Ninety-nine percent of childhood sexual abuse is done by groomers that fit a clear profile: Among the scale of forty-two characteristics and behaviors at the *Sexual Grooming Scale* (SGS-V) Jack had used all of them on me. I was an easy mark.

My beloved Gramps had died two years before, and my father and mother, had six young children, a full work life, and a busy household to run. We had recently moved homes and I was attending a new school. Familiar friends, teachers, and neighbors I had grown up with became distant. Jack ferreted out my need for love and attention and shrewdly preyed upon it.

My parents were trusting, generous, and assumed the best. Jack was invited to dinners and celebrated birthdays and holidays at our home. He had ways of making me feel that I was somebody important: spending time with me and my friends, even comparing me to some of what we kids considered the "coolest" movie stars of the 70s; he said that he admired my determination and wit. Above all, he told me that he loved me, and in my innocence and by my need, I believed him. Then, when alone with me, he'd cement the secret: "Son," he'd say in a hushed tone, a sincere look of his eyes into mine, one of his large, gnarled hands resting on my knee, "if anyone knew about this, Big Jack would go to the penitentiary." Unquestionably, he had my absolute loyalty. We were in this together.

I've been asked why, after telling him "No," and ending the abuse, did I continue to allow him in my life. That's the kind of question women in relationships with abusive men have had too often to withstand. It's hard to explain. The clearest explanation I have is that my child's capacity to receive and to give love was indeed sincere and pure, even though his warped intentions never were.

Still, I knew by something beyond words that what he was doing to us kids was hurtful and very wrong. On my fourteenth birthday on a camping trip with three other boys and him, sitting around the campfire, came another one of his attempts to coerce us. I exploded with rage. I told him that his tricking us and using us was wrong, that he was awful, and that from here on, it was over.

That night, with all of us together in a tent, my sleeping bag alongside his, through tears of hurt I told him, "Big Jack. You reminded me of my grandpa." And through his own tears of momentary regret he told me, "I could never be the man your grandfather was. He was a good man." I wanted to believe that Big Jack, like my Gramps, loved me for being the kid I was. Something within me knew that this could never be true.

Claiming

A targeted child of sexual abuse often lives in a matrix of confusion rife with pressure to hold secrecy, racked by disgust and shame. Even though victimized and trying to deflect the pain, I began searching for a deeper truth about who I was—beginning a journey to know my true self. I'd begin by detaching from him, once and for all, distancing myself from the hypocrisy and unwellness that Jack personified. I needed to find what I had been seeking from him, however, within myself.

Back then there were very few resources for understanding what had happened to us kids. We—the parents, neighbors, school authorities—were all in the dark. In my world, from childhood through adolescence, no one spoke about childhood sexual abuse. It wasn't in anyone's narrative except to say that there were creepy molesters, strangers on the prowl for unsuspecting children to grab. Otherwise, the topic was taboo. I, unfortunately, had sufficiently metabolized the stigmatization and cultural taboos around male homosexuality of the 1970s in the Mid-West U.S. I too was acutely aware of Jack's history and violent ideation, and of my father's fiery disposition. One gasoline, the other sparks: I kept them apart by harboring a potent secret within myself. In a situation well-beyond my developmental capacity to cope there was no way for me to accurately make sense of it. I was fermenting in chaos, mired in shame. Years later, my father told me that had I come to him then, he might have done something drastic out of a fierce need to protect me.

As part of my healing, I shared the essence of what had happened with my parents. Each was deeply affected—remorseful, filled with compassion for me, and outraged at the man they had once trusted. They stood beside me in my healing, offering not only their deep compassion but a quiet, enduring sense of responsibility for the pain we carried together.

A previous summer, on my fourteenth birthday when I had ended the abuse, I had begun the first steps of a formidable journey on the path to claiming my true Self. Still there was more to do. I went to Texas to begin shifting the power dynamic from my false self to my empowered Self—a self-initiation into a quest for aligning with my soul. Not to say that I was clear about my intention: although intuitively I knew. I was following my soul's longing guiding me to become who I was to be and to go beyond the grip of shame. I'd learn in my psychotherapy sessions that I had been suffering from the trauma of sexual abuse. I joined a men's survivor recovery group. And I became empowered as an advocate and educator for victims of sexual assault. I contacted the Matagorda County Texas Sheriff's Office and shared my experiences with Jack. They had strongly suspected it, but he thwarted their efforts by violently threatening the family and child who had agreed to testify in court.

A New Understanding

With time, healing, and perspective, I have come to view the abuse I experienced—along with its confusing twists and harsh lessons—as serving a higher purpose in my life. For many years, I could not comprehend how a child—any child—could be subjected to such hurt or anything like it. Over time, and after much inquiry, I understood the soul's path often appears extreme and confounding, yet it is precise in leading us toward the transformation we're ultimately seeking. My wound provided me with the right measure of concentration that would lead me to disconnect from dependency, moving me beyond victimhood and into a heart-centered way of being. This pain became the catalyst that awakened me to seek my true self within, no longer relying on external validation for inner peace.

Over time, I came to understand that while I had been victimized, I was not defined by it. This realization brought me to a critical choice: to either confront my pain and fight for my sense of self, or be consumed by it. This inner struggle, though fraught with challenges, was ultimately a gift, offering me the opportunity to choose resilience over defeat. Both choices carried unpredictability—twists, wrong turns, dead ends—but fighting for my true self promised acceptance, love, and a deeper connection to who I truly am. To succeed in this fight, I learned to listen closely to the quiet, buried whisperings of my soul's truth, long been overlooked.

Chapter Five

Kosha Power

If you were raised in the Western Hemisphere, particularly in the U.S., like many of us, you were probably taught a fairly limited way of referring to your physical body. The prevailing notions of the 2,400-year-old doctrine of mechanism views our bodies almost entirely as an amalgam of physical matter that will eventually deteriorate by the pull of gravity or fall prey to disease. Viewed as matter alone, the body's functions and its purpose are reduced to laws of cause and effect like any other kind of physical object or machine, as it might be. This is reductionist thinking rooted in a paradigm of fragmentation—a way of understanding the world by breaking and isolating actions, things, thoughts, and feelings into separate parts. It reduces outcomes to immediate, observable causes and effects, ignoring the hidden dynamics that exist within and between the parts. This method is central to the rational approach to knowledge, and it has limitations. Rooted in the philosophy of materialism, it insists that only what we can see, touch, measure, or quantify is real. But in doing so, it flattens the richness of our reality, leaving little room for the unseen, the felt, the intuitively known. It risks turning people away from their own wisdom, consciousness, emotion, and Spirit—the quiet dimensions through which so much of life is experienced and can be truly understood as part of our human experience.

Seen through the lens of materialism the body's sole purpose would be to assure safety, remain alive, move, and procreate for as long as it's feasible. And, like a machine when something goes wrong, it would be diagnosed, controlled, or fixed by medication, diet, and other procedures including surgery. A body would have a predictable life span, and after some point would fully depreciate, stop working, and die.

In his national bestselling and National Book Award-winning book, *How We Die*, Sherwin B. Nuland argues that mostly the underlying reason that physicians become specialists—researcher or clinician—no matter the sincerity of their regard for the sanctity for human life, is because they are absorbed by "the riddle of disease" and long to conquer it by solving puzzlements it presents to their inquisitive mind. Diagnosing and conquering disease is the driving force for many specialists. The intricacies of pathology captivate. Unfortunately, for the patient, many aspiring healers can become deterred by their own inability to cure and so they avoid the person. And while the diagnostic puzzle-solving approach brings us vast advances in nutrition, in treating injuries, and in disease prevention and cure, it also places unnecessary barriers to exploring the depth and complexity of our bodies, beyond its anatomy, as a vital resource of immense value to our human experience and spiritual evolution. Viewing the body solely as a machine might suggest it is self-contained and inanimate, but its true state of aliveness stems from something greater—a connection to the perfect intelligence. It carries the vitality of the Great within us.

The ancient Hindu philosophy *Vedānta* holds such a radically different view of the body. Beyond assuring our survival, mobility, and reproduction, the body is one of five essential layers of consciousness, or *koshas*, that make us up. The five koshas form a dynamically evolving, complex, interwoven system endlessly seeking to evolve and transcend into a whole being infused with the vitality of love. This invites a profound shift in perception for most Westerners by reframing what it means to be human through an integral lens, allowing us to see the self in a more complete sense and recognize more numerous possibilities for experiencing life as physical beings. Moreover, it offers a reliable map for exploring and discovering ourselves at our other levels of being human.

Annamaya Kosha: The Physical Body

*The body itself is a screen
to shield and partially reveal
the light that's blazing
inside your presence.*
—Rumi, translation by Coleman Barks

Annamaya Kosha is all about our physical bodies: skin, hair, muscles, bones, tendons, brain, and organs. It is the domain of our five senses that invites us to experience life in myriad ways. We navigate day-to-day movement and negotiate our survival by our bodies; by it we shape and influence the world around us. Our body brings sensation, it acts as a reservoir holding emotions and storing muscle memory. It grants us mobility to explore the Earth and to connect, touch and merge sensually with others. Our bodies also give us our felt sense of individuality and individual uniqueness essential for evolving our whole self. Just as no two blades of grass are the same, our senses serve a noble purpose—to help us make our way into the human domain—no body, no life here. There is no separation between our source and us. By attuning to the complex system of the body we are led to choices for embracing our authentic Self lending our contribution to the Great's universal quest of return to completeness.

Our most fundamental need, breathing, serves us far beyond simply keeping us alive. While the body is indeed physical, it is also a sacred vessel that houses the spark of divine light within us. By the breath traverses our renewal and connection to super-consciousness: fully embodied heightened states of awareness beyond ordinary consciousness acute intuition and cosmic insight to transcend the usual limitations of mind bridging us to higher liberating truth of unity. The body offers a passageway to the soul's discovery, its learning, its expression, and its pleasure.

Our physical form is a temporary vessel that provides the gift of resistance—gravity acting upon us imposing friction to ignite our powers of will pushing us to grow, strengthen, and achieve lasting impact beyond an otherwise ordinary life. So it is, by drubbing upon the anvil of Earth—gravity acting upon the body incurring friction and resistance—that we are compelled eventually to choose conscious action. Life does not move in a straight line; it presses, pulls, and shapes us through the fundamental forces of existence. Five Powers—presence, desire, surrender, love, and creation—act upon us as both weight and lift, tension and release. Presence roots us in the now, anchoring our awareness amidst life's ceaseless motion. Desire pulls us forward, the quiet hum of longing that stirs beneath the surface of all things. Surrender teaches us to yield, to soften against the hard edges of our resistance. Love, the most expansive of forces, dissolves separation, binding us to the great unfolding. And creation—our legacy—calls us to transmute the pressures of existence into something wholly new. Whenever we resist these forces, we struggle against the natural current of life, mistaking friction for failure, weight for burden. But when we engage them consciously, we begin to understand: the anvil is not to break us; it is to forge us. The very resistance we might curse is the necessary pressure to awaken us to our own becoming. Of course, by its signals of pain predicting its inevitable decline, we are constantly reminded of our limited time here—the body tells us that we won't last forever. It's through this awareness that we are driven to forge the immortal gold of our true nature.

Pranamaya Kosha: Life Force

In yogic philosophy, the act of breathing is closely connected with infusing life-force energy. Practicing pranayama elevates and balances vital energy within the body and creates new conditions of perception for waking up and transporting one into higher levels of awareness, eventually merging seamlessly with all of life—our own, others', and the Divine.

Pranayama, as described in ancient Hindu texts, such as the *Bhagavad Gita* and the *Yoga Sutras of Patanjali*, is the practice that unites body and mind with the immortal essence of our Higher Self. By focusing on the breath, we begin to sense the subtle presence of *prana*, the vital life force that is within us. Prana naturally seeks to intertwine with our aura, particularly around the heart (fourth chakra), the throat (fifth chakra), and the third eye (sixth chakra)—the centers of love, expression, and intuition. Failure to experience prana is due only to our own lack of awareness and knowledge of how to. Subtle prana can be felt throughout our entire being by consciously connecting to it with our breath through contemplative practices like meditation, guided imagery, yoga nidra, and hypnosis. What we are connecting to is the universal dynamics of the cosmos; and, as we do, we are gifting ourselves the highest expressions of love and intuition.

Kriya Yoga and *Holotropic Breathwork* are proven approaches for elevating consciousness through controlled, intentional guiding of the breath. Kriya Yoga, introduced to the West by Paramahansa Yogananda in the 1920s, is an ancient meditation technique that uses rhythmic breathing to foster a deep spiritual connection, inner peace, and a blissful union with the Divine. Yogananda described Kriya Yoga as a method that transforms oxygen into a life current that rejuvenates the brain and spine; by infusing ourselves with concentration of life force we gain passage into our highest ways of knowing, accessing our intuition, and ultimately, enabling spiritual oneness with the Great.

Through the breath, we experience our most elevated connection to Self and to the soul. Breath united with intention opens doors to our psyche and soul. Through the breath, we unlock profound emotional healing. Yogananda believed that through dedicated practice with the breath, one could reach higher spiritual states where consciousness merges with the Cosmic Spirit, achieving a state of "suspended animation"—remaining deeply connected to the spiritual realm even amidst the demands of daily life.

Manomaya: Mind

Manomaya where the senses and mind unite. The senses deliver the physical world to the mind, where it is transformed into thoughts, imagination, memories, and emotions. The concept of mind goes beyond typical understandings of it as consisting of merely intellect or rational. It's referring to a vast landscape we all can experience and enjoy—those of intuition, of sensations of all our pleasures and pains, our beliefs, desires, intentions, and of our emotions (emotions, though felt in the body, are rooted in mind).

Emotions tend to show up in one of two ways—as a reaction or as a response. When we're reacting, we're often caught up in the past, stuck in a state of mind that's pulling us away from the present moment. This can trap us, making it hard to make choices that best serve us. We can even become permanently trapped in some emotions, creating a fixed state, so much so that we confuse our true self with an emotional state. But when we respond, we're agile and connected to the here and now. We can see our choices more clearly and use our free will to navigate life-making choices that serve our Higher Selves alive with awareness.

When emotions and memories surface, meeting them with curiosity and openness allows us to heal and grow. By recognizing emotions as one part of our experience, we learn from them rather than being controlled by them. The more we release the past, the more we step into the natural flow of being fully present with ourselves. This frees up our mental space, allowing our emotions to become a source of wisdom rather than something that weighs us down.

Some emotions rush through loudly, others softly, but all of them move us in different ways. Over time, they settle into still, reflective pools, offering deeper insights into who we are.

Each emotion is meant to be felt and then released, much like water flowing through a freestone mountain stream—some gurgle loudly, some murmur softly, some gain momentum tumbling about, winding us up, bending us back, then swiftly through narrow chutes fall away freely. In time, all will eventually roll out smooth and still into quiet, reflective pools, to harbor new ways of knowing the Self in greater depth. Through expressing our emotions, we connect with our soul's purpose and direction. This happens when we open up and listen close.

Emotions, messengers of the heart, are ultimately for freeing the soul. They are our truth-tellers. Although our interpretation of them might fail us, they never lie. As we express our emotions, we breathe vitality. Experiencing all of them in the full range and making peace with the memories they carry must happen before there can be peace at death. The soul leaving the body fully at peace becomes a brilliant star in the heavens— unburdened, complete, luminous, and whole. Marilynne Robinson, in her reflections on generational legacy, spirit, and the beauty found in ordinary life, refers to the gentleness of the divine nestled within: "You can feel the silent and invisible life. All it needs from you is that you take care not to trample on it."

***

The following provides an opportunity for you to allow yourself to connect directly with your heart center. Begin by freeing your hands, then bring them together, heel to heel, in front of your chest, at your heart space, your Anahata. Take two full, calming breaths. Allow your eyes to softly focus as you read, or perhaps, ask someone close to you to read the following to you.

Become aware of your breathing, noticing each inhale and exhale. If your mind begins to wander, bring it back to focus on the pace and depth of your breathing.

Notice the rhythm as your chest rises and falls with each inhalation and exhalation. Be aware of the slight pauses between each inhale and exhale. Notice these natural pauses for three more breaths, the ebb and flow of air coming into you and leaving you effortlessly. You don't need to do anything else. Simply observe your breath coming in and going out.

Now imagine your breath as if it is coming directly into and going out of your heart space, your Anahata. It does so with perfect ease. With curiosity, explore the possibility of a spark emanating from within your heart space. Allow your imagination to show you that. Take a few more breaths as you do this.

How bright is the light within your heart space? What color is it? Is it more than one color? How much does the light move within you? How does it feel to be aware of the spark inside you in this moment? Notice whatever arises without judgment or expectation. Invite your mind's eye to follow it and explore sensations that might come into your awareness. In this moment as you breathe softly, allow yourself to reconnect compassionately to yourself, opening to your speck of divine light within you.

Now set an intention to let go of any doubts you might be having and extend your willingness even further. I encourage you to speak gently to the light that is within you. Ask it anything. You might start with a simple query, such as, "In this moment what do I need to know about myself?" Pause for an answer; it might come as a word or two, perhaps an image, a sound, or simply a notion or feeling. What are you sensing? Another question to consider: "What is the most loving thing

I can do for myself at this time in my life?" Again, pause for an answer; it might come as a word or two, perhaps an image, a sound, or a feeling. What are you sensing? You can answer any other questions that might come to mind. Pause to receive answers.

If you find yourself stuck or unsure, ask for a sign to come to you in the future, at a time when you're ready. Pledge to welcome it when it arrives and be patient as you wait. To finish, express your appreciation and gratitude. Allow your eyes to open fully and your hands to move from your heart space.

What did you notice? How challenging or simple was it? How new or familiar? What did you learn or learn again? If you're open to doing it again, look for ways to include it in any daily practice you have, such as meditation, yoga, and prayer, before sleeping at night, or when waking up in the morning, or simply while taking a stroll. These ways of connecting are always available to you—it's the gateway to your soul, which is always wise, welcoming, and full of love to give you.

Expressing our core emotional truths reinvigorates the freedom to be and alertness to find our path to our truth. Let nothing you have done be in vain. At the surface it might not appear so or didn't work out that way, every experience each of us has had, and will have, share a desire to alleviate pain. Personal freedom and its aliveness start with showing compassion for ourselves as we face our memories, the pleasant ones and those that are painful.

Inner healing attunes us to our unique resonance of longing that travels the chords of our pain. Rumi, refers to the intelligence behind pain—that the hurting want of pain hears its cure like a child and discovers that the cure for the pain is found within the pain.

Though we might stare within our void, at the very origin of our pain, we may not see it. Yet the closer and more attentive we are of ourselves, offering compassion and forgiveness, we find within us a new and formidable healing hunger awaits. Listening to our soul's longing, choosing to go inward, and meeting our pain—often hidden, embedded beneath layers of fear—though not ordinarily our first choice—is a courageous and loving act. The effects are cumulative: Each time we turn towards our hurting want new healing pathways are revealed, the self expands, and wisdom of the soul blossoms.

Vijnanamaya Kosha: Wisdom

Vijnanamaya harbors our curiosity and intuition that leads us to our most credible insights and intuition and to richer understanding of ourselves, others, and the world around us. This is our wisdom sheath that endlessly seeks cosmic awareness and aims to guide us on our spiritual journey, helping us to heal our wounds and discover how to truly love and be loved.

Within each of us lies a complex tapestry of identities, formed and shaped by necessity in past lives and in our current one. These identities—our inner children of various ages, the inner critic (sometimes there's more than one), the responsible adult self who wants to make sensible decisions, and the compassionate, creative, free-spirited, and loving adult—sometimes have conflicting desires and goals. Despite these differences, our mind possesses the remarkable ability to integrate them into a unified sense of self—a harmonious *me, mine, I*—that forms the foundation of a healthy, balanced ego.

Each stage of our life—infancy, childhood, adolescence, young adulthood, mature adulthood, and beyond—contributes to the formation of our ego. Some parts coexist peacefully, while others are still finding their place. Over the years, we've learned to ignore some of them by burying them away. Although they're hidden, they never go away, they'll all have some influence on us.

A compassionate ego is accommodating, pure in its intention to serve all aspects of who we are. It integrates all of our parts into a unified whole, and we become more complex, adaptable, creative, and flexible. Life becomes more engaging and enjoyable.

It's fully committed to the success of our soul, acting as the good servant-ego fulfilling its role by supporting our awakening. It becomes like an orchestra conductor, syncopating all our identities into one harmonious performance. It knows that our great music originates from the Self, influenced by the soul, not the other way around.

As we heal old patterns of thinking and embrace what we've learned, we transcend ordinary consciousness and open the door to bliss.

Our ego carries on identities, needs, and drives that over the years we have learned to ignore and deny. They remain buried under layers of sediments. Some co-exist in harmony, while others are still re-positioning and morphing into a coherent form. When we have a compassion-driven, stable ego unifying and integrating all our identities into a holistic whole, we become more complex, adaptable, resourceful, creative, and flexible; life becomes much more enjoyable and engaging. Such a compassionate ego is pure in its intention to serve, fully invested in the success of our soul. It is a servant-ego fulfilling its intended role, supporting our awakening by responding to the influence of our Self and our soul. That it is an effect of the soul, not the other way around,

To complete steps to a healthy ego—by healing habitual ways of the mind, including what we've learned—ordinary consciousness is transcended, and bliss is made possible.

Anandamaya Kosha: Bliss

Anandamaya, the most interior of the koshas, the bliss sheath surrounding and holding the *Atman*, our center of higher consciousness that is a spark of divine, universal, eternal, and immutable essence, imbuing each of us with absolute goodness, truth, and beauty. It is not limited by individuality, body, or mind and, it is endlessly seeking bliss in reunion with the Great. The true self (or Higher Self) is a fragment of it.

Bliss refers not to a mere emotion but to a different order of reality that encompasses feelings of extraordinary well-being, of profound peace, serenity, cosmic unity, and rapture. Bliss is a state of deep peace, immense joy, and pervading love. It is a revelation of our connection to the Divine, showing us that we are inseparable from our source, which is pure goodness, truth, and beauty. It offers us powerful forces for healing by remembering—rejoining the fragmented parts of our soul splintered by wounding inflicted upon us in life—beyond abuse, illness, loss, and tragedy.

Another way to appreciate willfulness for experiencing enduring blissfulness, transcendental unity of becoming one with Oversoul, is through the rigor of scientific inquiry. The earlier mentioned, neuroscientist and physician Andrew Newberg has extensively studied the quest for such spiritual enlightenment—that anyone of us dedicated enough can know—by the study of "neurotheology": the relationship between the brain (namely parietal lobe, limbic, thalamus, and frontal lobes) and spiritual experience. Newberg has identified a sequence of five distinct steps. First, a Sense of Oneness—connecting to something greater and more profound than the self; second, a Sense of Intensity—powerful immersion into love and inspiring pursuit of transcendent reality; third, a Sense of Clarity—emotional or cognitive insight into one's true existence; fourth is a Sense of Wonder involving surrender of the ego to the mystical; finally, there comes a Sense of Transformation evoking a lasting shift in meaning, purpose, and acceptance of mortality, often accompanied by the absence of fearing death. Newberg's findings suggest that the foundational step in the search for oneness begins with the brain's capacity to experience profound feelings of love, which catalyze the journey toward spiritual awakening and transcendence.

Most of us experience Atman only fleetingly, as a flash of light in our mind's sky, or perhaps when deep in meditation, or falling asleep, heightened sexual experiences, or other kinds of peak experiences. It comes to us often during sleep. Those who had a near-death experience have reported an immense, indescribable sensation of love.

Hindu scholar, Sri Aurobindo, who has co-authored with Mirra Alfassa extensively about the Atman said that "Its action is like a searchlight showing up all that has to be changed in the nature; it has in it a flame of will, insistent on perfection. Its will is for the divination of life, the expression through it of a higher Truth, its dedication is to the Divine and Eternal." Its sightline pierces the veils of illusion so that we can come to know ourselves as an indispensable and unique part of the universal whole. It is the source of infinite wisdom, the *Secret Teacher* within, for guiding the soul to wholeness. Aurobindo and Alfassa discuss the immortal aspect of the soul that will continue across lifetimes. The *psychic being* is a portion of our soul within us, that presides over our normal consciousness and will serve us through many lifetimes until it is fully awakened.

What's Soul?

The ancient Hindu texts, such as the *Bhagavad Gita*, and the *Upanishads*, describe the soul, or *jivātma*, as an active learner seeking wisdom by evolving through lives in the body, and in the time between them. The soul, our Secret Teacher, journeys through life, accumulating karma and cycling through birth, death, and rebirth in its quest for liberation from separation. Meanwhile, it remains bound to separateness, tethered to our physical and subtle bodies, working through the limitations of ego, mind, and the five senses. In the meantime, bound by separateness, tied to our physical and subtle energetic bodies, it must navigate by way of the limits of ego, mind, and the five senses. Even so, the soul's reach of consciousness is vast, touching universal planes of mind, life and matter far beyond senses and personality. It is seeking to ultimately release from attachment to our learned habitual, compulsive, and reactive attitudes, beliefs, and behaviors. The soul's highest goal is to realize that it and *Atman* are ultimately one and the same and to rejoin it for eternity.

Robert Schwartz, author of two award-winning books, *Your Soul's Plan* and *Your Soul's Gift*, also speaks of an "inner being"—a mysterious entity that interfaces between one's personality and soul. In Schwartz's works, the soul is portrayed as an eternal, spiritual essence that carefully plans significant life experiences before birth. These experiences, including challenges and hardships, are chosen to foster personal and ontological growth: healing, and the evolution of love and compassion, and aligning with the soul's ultimate purpose. Tim Laurence, in his book, *The Hoffman Process*, similarly speaks of a dedicated inner being as "Spiritual Self" our divine guide, that assists us in healing and growth, helping us move beyond our learned, neurotic ways of thinking and being.

As we explore these concepts further, I will refer to the soul conceptually as the combination of the psychic being and jivātma. In addition to occasional use of Atman, I will use the terms *Self* or *Higher Self* for describing the superconscious spirit within, and I'll use the lowercase *self* when referring to our ego or personality. Generally, when referring to the source of all creation—Brahmin, God, Source, Great Spirit—I'll often use the terms *the Great* or *the Divine*.

Soul's Path

Each person is a mystery in possession of an exquisite gem of brilliant facets to become revealed and cherished. Each of us is a captivating, fluctuating entity with five dynamic koshas uniting to fulfill the same ultimate purpose—to awaken the grandeur and merge together as one divine being, forever.

The body offers you a connection to your Higher Self. Here's a simple way to quickly access that. In this moment, pause and tune in to its subtle presence by starting with observing the blinking of your eyelids. So simple and fluid: in an instant a complete opening and closing, a momentary blur between refocusing your eyes reopen to light. Watch your blinking eyelids a handful of times. Then attune to vibrations of any sound that might be entering your ears. What do you hear? How does it feel to hear differing kinds of sound? What's pleasing or, annoying? Turn your attention to your breath. Another reflexive action, that's keeping you alive. At your next few inhales, notice air coming into you, follow it as it passes down your throat into your lungs. How much is coming into you? How much stays and how much leaves you? What happens if you interrupt your breath? One of the body's many gifts is sensations to help you engage with yourself authentically. There is nothing more real, or dependable, than the language of your body. It is a conduit of soul.

The soul is uncuttable, unpierceable, ever evolving, and immortal. It seeks to know and learn from experience within realms of time and space. Gravity and resistance are essential for achieving its fully evolved final state in becoming reunited with the Great. Atman, the splintered diamond essence held within the body, intent on returning to a state of eternal bliss, acts like a magnet drawing us towards the Great. The Higher Self is our Secret Teacher and provides some poignant imagery for our diamond essence, as well, a diamond: a vast diamond that is within each person, a foot long and adorned with a thousand facets hidden as if beneath layers of dirt and tar. It is the soul's sacred duty to cleanse each one of them, allowing the light of the diamond to shine brilliantly in its full rainbow of colors. We each have ahead a journey of purification to reveal our inner beauty and boundless potential, and to illuminate our unique light within and among the world around us. Most of the time I envision that our soul on its purification journey is nourished by all our experiences and is endlessly gleaning wisdom from everything that we experience. It uses our senses to perceive first-hand information: it sees through our eyes, hears with our ears, smells through our nose, tastes with our tongue, and touches and experiences pleasures of sensation through our skin. For our lifetime, and by our bones, it remains firmly rooted upon the Earth.

There are two paths by which the soul travels—one of destiny and another of free will. The soul, imbued with sacred vitality, is offered guidance to grow and must act of its own free will to do so.

This is a two-way relationship, too. When our whole being is aligned, our soul shepherds us with clear intention and infuses purposefulness into everything we do. Ultimately it ventures, discovers, learns, and gathers wisdom to complete its state of longing to complete our journey of purification to fully illuminate our diamond essence.

***

Longing is for leading us from dead ends of denial and confusion to a new road of reclaiming our childlike innocence and surrendering to the enormously powerful, yet subtle, unfamiliar power that we carry. Your soul awaits quietly and with patience, to assert its power and guide you on your life's course. It calls to you by its subtle whispers, teaching you to listen for its guidance. It is here now. Experience it by pausing, to turn inward; speak these words softly to yourself.

Please show me the way into my truth. Bring me further into my authenticity so that I may intimately know my essence and directly experience my own inner beloved light. Teach me how to attend to you as you deserve. In this lifetime, I want to rejoin all aspects of who I am. Teach me how to know and to align with my soul's true purpose for this lifetime. I am learning; I need to be taught and taught again. I promise, here and now, to return whenever is needed and to further my learning. Teach me to hear you, to know the messages that you convey to me, the unique diction of your language be they by words, by sensation, or by quiet knowing. I am ready now, and I vow to continue becoming more ready to be a student of you, my soul.

Whatever comes will come in terms of kindness. As you listen closely, feel your bravery and the power of your humble tenderness. Know that you are your own hero. Heroes are not made; they become, just as you are becoming by seeking cadence with your soul. In doing so, you reconnect with your innermost being and harmonize all layers of yourself with your soul.

Chapter Six

Vitalities and Realities

As physical and spiritual beings, our vitality, our life force, manifests in three distinct forms. One is formative, grounding for shaping our physical surroundings and ensuring our safety and survival, while another consumes experiences to learn from them by urging us to reject stagnation and to grow at the level of the personality. The third is ethereal and fuels our spiritual journey. They work separately, and together to weave complex changes.

Formative

Formative vitality works in dimensions of space and time, subject to gravity and mass. Day-to-day, it helps keep us physically and psychologically safe by conveying instinctual information and keeping us attuned to where, what, and who we are and when and what we need to keep ourselves alive and well. Like built-in radar waves, formation vitality scans our environment to navigate threats and opportunities.

Formative vitality is also for supporting an optimal version of our personality in support of our soul's journey to ensure that it acquires specific experiences, learning new lessons needed for our evolution.

The ego works from formative vitality, optimally functioning as a mediator between all constituents of our personality. Like a skillful stage director, it expertly coordinates the performances of life with sensibility and grace. Without it, our efforts can become awkward, aimless, and wasteful. But when we over-rely on ego there is infectiveness. An outsized, unbridled and self-important ego will seek to dominate all other aspects of the self. It's preoccupation with watching out for threats to its authority, even from the very soul of one's being can be exhausting. It might even go so far as to attempt a rewrite of the script about our life's purpose, produce and direct the show, and become the sole lead actor masterminding its own durability, positioning itself as a pseudo-soul master of all things spiritual. The louder voice of ego impedes the subtler calling of our soul. The ego presents as the object of our being instead of subject to it—perceiving itself to be the cause, and reason, for our existence creating all kinds of existential confusion. It's like we're attempting to live two identities—a false one behind the wheel and the true one in the trunk. Then, instead of embracing our longing and inviting mystery into what's unknown, the ego perceives a threat and tries to shut things down. Ego is confused and frightened.

The true seat of the ego resides at the mezzanine of formative vitality—the nesting space of our physical well-being, and a bit beyond. The ego was brought into material existence by the soul to assist in its evolution (and, not the other way around). Graduate professor and psychologist Annabelle Nelson explains that the ego serves this purpose by linking basic self-awareness with the present time:

"I exist here and now," or put another way, "I exist, therefore I am."

In this way, the ego helps us to recognize our individuality—our distinction from one another and from the world around us. From Nelson's way of seeing it, "This process eventually leads to a realization that the ego is not the same as the self," which further leads to capacity to differentiate between our ego self and our spiritual self and soul.

But when the ego grows frightened and lost, it pulls inward, clinging to survival. In that tight grip, it begins to seize control, building walls to shield itself—walls that quietly dampen growth, connection, and grace. The ego turns away from its true role—not as a guide for the soul's daily unfolding, but as a sentinel guarding its own fragile ground. It clings to a new belief: "I exist just to exist."

An unchecked, out-sized ego craves more—more money, more houses, more cars, more land, more prestige, more power. It reaches outward, seeking control over every direction, every dimension, even the lives of others. But the chase ends in hollowness, a kind of emotional vacancy, and a weariness that echoes hollowly through the soul. True peace doesn't come from accumulation; it comes from thawing what's long been frozen beneath fear—from this life and, perhaps, from ancient wounds carried across lifetimes. Only there can the ego's false story behind the craving begin to unravel.

Metabolic

Metabolic forces of the soul usher in renewal by roiling our consciousness, unsealing ingrained, staid limitations, of our ancient burdens allowing our good, true, and beautiful essence to shine.

Fire radiates heat and light as it draws oxygen and consumes combustible fuel. In the wild, fire brings life back from death by transforming inert material into nourishment for new growth. Since our beginnings, human beings have relied on the power of fire to provide warmth, light, cooking abilities, land clearing, metal crafting, waste incineration, rituals, and cremation pyres. Each year natural fires consume millions of acres of forest. However, attending to the essential balance between the land and humans, Indigenous peoples have long practiced intentional cultural burning that involves strategically placing controlled fires to mitigate wide-scale destruction, consume decay, and invite new growth within an ecosystem. But fire must keep a fine balance. Without oxygen and fuel, it will consume itself, smother, and die out.

Similarly, each of us holds within a power of metabolic force that can either destroy or purify. The trick is keeping it in balance. However, out of fear of our own power we sometimes attempt to suppress our fire from awakening ourselves to open beyond the level of the egoic personality.

Ethereal

Ethereal vitality is everywhere all around us. We know it by the changing of the seasons, by the phases of the moon, by storms, hurricanes, tornadoes, and earthquakes. The essence of the universe lies in the delicate balance between opposing forces: yin and yang. We see it in wind, lightning, and ever-changing clouds. It is present in the flight of birds and butterflies, and it flows through our bodies with each beat of our hearts and with every breath we take. Ethereal reveals itself when we heal from illness or injury. It is present at moments of birth and upon acceptance at death. In our emotions lie its fluctuations and fluidity—their arrival, timing, intensity, and manifestation of feelings in our hearts. We know its longing by our yearning for inner peace, beyond materialistic desires, and in our striving to love and be loved.

The secret to quenching the thirst for ethereal vitality lies in embracing stillness and opening ourselves to knowing our purpose in moments of simply being. With curiosity, the self opens to discovery, reflection, and understanding of its true place and purpose in this lifetime. It is the first to surround the Atman, our eternal center of higher consciousness. Inspiring ethereal energy, striving for total consciousness springs from Anandamaya Kosha, the most interior kosha. It often has an unexpected liberating effect on our past experiences by drawing us into our spaciousness within, reviving and leading to the void within—the quantum field of knowledge accessible to our soul. It is the vibration upon which our longing transmutes our hearts.

Ethereal energy, a hidden power awaiting our connection, can be summoned by us. Essence of Great consciousness, it is described by prolific near-death experience scholar and author Kenneth Ring as "all-encompassing unconditional love of radiant light," a force beyond human comprehension. But we can experience it. It seeks to manifest and grow within all living things; it wants each of us to engage with it. It is in search of enlightenment.

***

Consider taking a moment now to experience your vital ethereal energy. Begin by pausing it and welcoming it as you might a trusted friend or loved one. Ask it to enter your heart space— your fifth chakra within your chest area. Speak directly to it. Feel its presence within your body. Encourage it to expand outward to encircle your whole body. Notice its color. Notice in this moment, as you breathe slowly and deeply, this loving ethereal energy vibrating in cadence within you, as it forever has been. At some level you have known this far better than anything else you have known in your lifetime.

Follow it now as you breathe steadily, deeply. It flows and expands only to the degree that you invite it to do so. In this moment consider inviting it to swell within you however you wish. You determine its strength within yourself. You direct its course. It comes from the purity of your soul.

To fully immerse yourself in the deepening experience ahead, I recommend freeing your hands or asking a friend or partner to read the following to you, allowing your eyes to softly focus.

Imagine that within you, at the center of your chest, there in your heart space, is a soft green light pulsating in cadence with the beating of your heart. Take a moment to breathe into it. As you breathe notice the rhythm of that pulsating green light within you. Pause, and breathe this way three or four more times. Then, with your next few breaths notice how the ethereal green light responds to your breath inhaling and exhaling.

You are breathing effortlessly. You are imbued with gentle, purifying ethereal light feeling kindness and compassion that is inherent within you. This is your true nature. Allow it to fill you. Feel the vitality of your own kindness within you as your own loving vibrations radiate from your heart space outward, and throughout your body. It flows down your shoulders. This green ethereal light takes on a warm golden hue now as it spreads over your shoulders and across the base of your neck. Then it flows down your arms and out your fingertips. The pulsation of kindness within you is becoming wider and stronger as you continue to breathe into your heart space. Notice how natural your own light feels within you. It is as if it has been with you your entire existence, and it has. This is your natural ethereal vitality.

To deepen your experience, continue to direct your breathing within yourself upward and outward, following your inhaled breath down your arms and out your fingertips. Then follow it as it continues to flow out to cradle your neck with warmth. It then spreads throughout your face, behind your eyes, and out through the top of your head. You are connecting with your own ethereal vitality. Absorb it as it comes effortlessly. There is an endless supply. You are simply allowing it to be. Follow your breath in and, then out. You are swelling with your own ethereal vitality. It is yours to invite into your consciousness at any time. When you feel ready speak some parting words knowing that you and your ethereal vitality are always one.

What did you notice? How challenging or simple was that to do? How new or familiar was it? What did you learn? If you're open to doing it again, look for ways to include it in any daily practice that you have, such as meditation, yoga, and prayer, before sleeping at night, or when waking up in the morning, or simply while taking a walk. These ways of connecting are always available to you—they are the gateway to your soul, which is always wise, welcoming, and full of love to give you.

Five Realities of Higher Mind

A reality of mind is a state of awareness that, to our cognitive minds, seems mostly separate from other forms of awareness, yet serves as the foundation from which all others are recognized. The Five Realities form a system of soul praxis, designed to strengthen our vitality through a continuous cycle of action, awareness, and reflection—followed by integrating new ways of being so that knowledge is embodied in action. Practicing each reality requires ongoing commitment: to remain conscious, to engage in life with purpose, and to embrace the soul's transformation.

By opening to what is in any moment—even in the midst of a storm—a person embraces the first reality, acceptance: *I wish this wasn't happening, and yet it is.* Recognizing that one is not a victim of circumstances but an empowered being with choice is the second reality, responsibility: *Somehow, someway, I brought this experience into my life, and so it's mine to navigate.* Choosing to be fully present with all thoughts and emotions, engaging with the moment in real time, is the third reality, presence: *I choose to be here now, to fully engage, and to seek guidance from the Divine, including my soul.* Seeking to understand the complexity of experience in all its dimensions is the fourth reality, active learning: *What is this asking me to know? How must I be to learn what I need?* When the experience passes and one pauses to reflect, honor, and uncover its deeper lessons, they enter the fifth reality, wisdom: *I am here to experience and learn enduring truths in service of my soul.* Each of these five realities is guided by the soul's longing. The soul calls us to engage them and seeks to master them all.

Each time that we follow our commitment to evolve ourselves, sacred transformative opportunities come to us. Whenever we open to them, we not only honor the inherent wisdom that comes from living in struggle, but we also empower ourselves to emerge from adversity with newfound strength, wisdom, and compassion. Viktor E. Frankl, a Holocaust survivor of Nazi concentration camps and founder of Logotherapy, holds that the quest for fulfilling our life's meaning is the most compelling motivational force that we possess.

You may find it helpful to explore the belief that every reality you encounter serves a purpose: to teach and support the growth of your soul. To stay connected to this truth, I find it grounding to recite and reflect on words that came to me during an immersive experience: Experiences are skins that I shed to reveal the majesty of my Soul.

Chapter Seven

Omega Point

Pando, Latin for "I spread," is the name of the largest of all single-seed aspen clones. A massive organism that dates to the end of the last Ice Age, Pando has birthed over 40,000 individual trees linked by an ever-expanding root system endlessly self-generating, perpetuating its own genetic material identical to every other part. Rising high into the sky, aspens thrive and grow at elevations of 12,000 feet. In harmony with its environment aspen's smooth, powdery white bark dapples with grayish scars resembling human eyes. In summertime, heart-shaped leaves murmur in the softest breezes as they convert sunlight into energy by absorbing carbon dioxide from the air above and nutrients and water from the ground below. They are filled with aromatic compounds imbued with healing properties. In autumn the spectacle of their brilliant amber leaves light up the Rocky Mountains.

Human civilizations across eons have thrived through existential connection: investigating our existence, inventing new ways to survive and thrive, healing emotional vulnerabilities, and ever-expanding our individual and collective consciousness. We nourish one another by sharing a drink from the springs of universal wisdom within ourselves. Our individual quest for life resonates with the quest of those around us, creating a ripple effect that amplifies our hope. The rhythm of lives possessed with renewal and purpose nourishes the great collective spirit. We create and we find stability in each other. Our branches reach out and our leaves draw in light to activate us. By embracing one another with compassion, we provide nutrients of inspiration and spread healing properties of mutual love. We thrive by evolving together: the consciousness we share vitalizes each of us and all of us. There is no shortage of it. Our collective wisdom is awakened by the power of mutual compassion infusing vigor and strength into every part of our individual and collective aliveness.

Undivided Wholeness

One offshoot of materialism, atomic physics theory, proposes that we and all other objects in the universe, came into being by random occurrence and remain interrelated primarily by location, time, and happenstance. Everything in the universe, including consciousness, arises from material substances. This viewpoint aligns with the belief that atoms, as the fundamental building blocks of matter, govern all physical processes.

But one of the most influential theoretical physicists of the 20th century, David Bohm, developed a mathematical theory of physics which finds something considerably different — that both an implicit and an explicit order are active within all matter; that particles are acting both separately and together in flow, endlessly seeking novel ways of movement within a predominant order implicitly seeking unity. Bohm called this "undivided wholeness in flowing movement" and suggested that this reveals the need to perceive the universe in seamless unity "where the world is an undivided whole, in which all parts of the universe are merging and uniting into one totality." Existence is a boundless flow where all elements intertwine and merge, contributing to a wholeness beyond comprehension. This view transcends striving to figure out the causation and physical properties of separate objects. Instead, it focuses on the fluid movements that give rise to matter. In this way, mind and matter are intertwined, two facets of an unbroken continuum endlessly forming new patterns in a never-ending stream of possibilities. With this perception, we can embrace the interconnectedness of existence and relinquish the divisive tendencies of our limited atomic viewpoint.

Pulsation of growth and expansion beats fiercely at the heart of the universe itself. Luminary, anthropologist and explorer, Pierre Teilhard de Chardin, writing in the 1920s, was captivated by this profound truth. With impassioned fervor, he delved into the mysteries of human evolution and the boundless potential of our cosmos. He called it *noogenesis*: a cosmic force coursing through every atom and organism, infusing them with vitality and purpose. de Chardin envisioned this force as a radiant web of consciousness, interconnecting all life forms and propelling them toward a single transcendent goal.

Pursuing Omega

Omega Point is the ultimate convergence, where individual souls and collective consciousness meld into a symphony of unity and understanding where barriers of race, culture, and nationality dissolve in the radiant glow of shared humanity in a world where human diversity is not a source of division but that each uniqueness is a wellspring of strength and solidarity contributing to greater complexity for ascending higher levels of existence. This means that, instead of exploiting our differences, we are to celebrate them and join with their power to bind us together as one evolving global family.

The pursuit of Omega Point is nothing short of a sacred calling—a generative quest for transforming fear into courage, ignorance into wisdom, hatred into love, and conflict into peace. It's fueled by the fire of our shared craving for a nobler world—a world where the power and warmth of Omega Point ignites the hearts of humanity and illuminates the path toward a future where peace reigns supreme.

Before analytical thinking wins us over, at some level, all human beings know Omega to be true. I had an inkling of it when I was about eight years old and, on a summer day, lying on the grass at a nearby park, the notion behind this poem came to me:

When a young boy I sensed It,
by strangers I saw It,
and I wondered:
Why I, why them?
Why not me, as they?
Said It,
"You are them and they you."

Bliss

Within every human heart resides its own blazing Omega Point—a journey unique for each of us. Our soul calls us to the sacred duty of awakening, inviting us to discover and pursue our true purpose—recognizing that the very act of pursuing it is, in itself, living aligned with our purpose. Echoing the wisdom of Joseph Campbell, the eminent philosopher and explorer of cultural mythology—we are urged to release the grip of our preconceived plans and courageously embrace the unknown path that beckons us. Campbell's words resound with passion and urgency:

"I say, follow your bliss, and don't be afraid. Doors will open where you didn't know they were going to be."

Then, reminding us that we are not alone in our quest and that the heroes of myth and legend have trodden this path before us, illuminating the way, Campbell said:

> *Furthermore, we have not even to risk the adventure alone, for the heroes of all time have gone before us. The labyrinth is thoroughly known. We have only to follow the thread of the hero's path, and where we had thought to find an abomination, we shall find a god. Where we had thought to travel outward, we will come to the center of our own existence. And where we had thought to be alone, we will be with all the world.*

Life in the body is an act of sheer bravery, making us all, by nature, heroic. Across time—past, present, and future—every soul encounters challenges or danger, sometimes even extreme threats: illness, harm, adversity, assault, discrimination, injustice, aging, scarcity, struggle, mortality, natural catastrophe, and countless others. And yet, we remain to prevail.

When we dare to release the need to predict and control, when we kindle the flames of our Spirit essence, we not only nourish our own souls, but we contribute to the collective uplifting of humanity. We become interconnected threads in the tapestry of existence, bound together by empathy and mutual concern. Sharing in each other's joys and sorrows, our individual journeys are intertwined with the greater story of humanity's evolution. When we embrace our uniqueness we become beacons of light, guiding others toward their own Omega Point. Together, we rise, fueled by the fire of our collective longing for truth, meaning, and connection. And in this shared journey, we discover that our truest fulfillment lies not in isolation, but in the vibrant tapestry of human experience, where every thread will become woven with love, courage, and boundless possibility. What might appear at first a daunting crisis, for many of us is actually a thrust into an acute opportunity to declare an authentic commitment to, paraphrasing visionary Lynne Twist, invent new ways of being that we haven't known before, find resources we didn't even know existed, create relationships where within every disappointment, every heartbreak, every breakdown lay the opportunity for a breakthrough to an evolutionary leap in life. As we'll explore in more detail through stories of five courageous people, we may at one time or another in our lives receive, what Twist refers to as, "a call to create."

***

All of us, you and I too, are wonders to be explored, multi-faceted, endlessly evolving mysteries awaiting our own discovery. Tunneling into the mystery of your depths with curiosity will reveal intrinsic brilliance. In this way, the purpose of living becomes clear, and following it, natural; the right and real ways in life become instinctive. The wisdom behind the soul's longing is the Great summoning of the self to the gestation of life's purpose. To be living on one's true purpose is to be living from one's heart. A hero knows their path has heart because they are at one with it, experiencing the clarity, the peace, and the pleasure in traversing its length.

Consider taking this moment to open to the heart of your life purpose. One way to start is by bringing the heels of your hands together and placing them at your heart center, each pinky finger, thumb, and heel of your hands connected to its opposite, and with your index, middle, and ring fingers extended and apart forming an opened blossom. Inhale a full complete breath and release it slowly.

With each breath you take in and each you release, envision a stream of your favorite color of light coming to you. It is effortlessly moving in cadence with the beating pulse of vitality within you. Begin by opening to your light, breathing in and allowing it to saturate your heart space. Then, slow and steady, watch as it spreads out and permeates all your being. With your next deep breath, it moves beyond your immediate physical body to your outer-most perimeter—your kosha of bliss. Your color fills your kosha bliss. You are radiating with your own love and light. Breathe it in.

Your light will always direct you to what is best for you to know. In this moment allow the leading edge of your light to guide you by its graceful movement. As you draw in a next deep full breath it moves into your heart space. Follow it there beneath your hands, as it fills you with love and warmth. Breathe that in. It moves then to the base of your throat and cleanses you. Breathe in its cleansing power. As you do, you feel as if you are waking up from a deep slumber, ready to reveal rare precious truths that may even have been kept hidden within you. Your light now moves gently to the space between your eyes at the level of your eyebrows. Your urge to know grows more robust and more inviting. There your light brings forth even more brilliance of your color. Breathe in the gratitude of knowing there is beauty and wisdom within you. It is filling you with knowing who you are and what you are here to do in this lifetime. Assure yourself that you are ready to know your truth. That you are open to knowing the purpose of your life. Vow to stay open to anything that you might have kept locked away inside, those may be asking to be revealed to you. Willingness to know your truth will grow and expand as you continue turning inward with self-compassion and self-appreciation. Breathe in that truth. You are feeling self-kindness, universally connected to the Great and present to yourself and your soul. Breathe in your connection to them.

Take this moment to reflect briefly upon the following prompts. Let this be a fully intuitive process. Follow the first thought that comes to mind and when it passes go on to the next one. When completed make notes if you'd like. The whole experience should take no more than thirty minutes. Begin by taking a few deep breaths.

I am most peaceful and at ease when...
I'd like to be ...
I am most engaged in life when...
I feel grateful to be alive whenever I ...
I am fulfilled and inspired by ...
I experience mastery when ...
I find joy and pleasure in ...
I feel great appreciation for myself because...
I was born in this specific time in history in order to...
Take another deep, full breath and exhale with a sigh.

Each of us, by experiencing life on Earth, have accepted a sacred invitation to contribute our uniqueness. We do so by surrendering to our own natural flow and by becoming our authentic self and living our purpose. Though our paths may differ, the essence remains the same: releasing the limiting belief that we are separate from one another and committing to reunite our self with our soul and the Great All That Is. In this sacred union, we fulfill the purpose of our existence. Every experience—whether drenched in pain or joy, sorrow or hope—holds the potential to elevate our soul's journey, if we are willing to embrace, forgive, reflect, and learn from them. In doing so, we weave these moments into the fabric of our own unique wisdom. Then our traumas and tragedies are no longer mere misfortunes but serve as portals to an ever-expanding consciousness within our soul and fall in rhythm with the eternal dance toward Omega Point.

Life's endless, seemingly random, fluxes, and flows bend us toward unity. All of us, and whatever we do, matters. What we do, we do as one. None of us is truly separate. As Martin Luther King, Jr. pointed out, "We may have all come in on different ships, but we're in the same boat now."

Chapter Eight
Living Transformations

Once Again
I am White now learning,
before then, Black and learned.
I am a man now learning,
before, a woman who learned,
. . . as we will once again,
ring-a-ring o' roses,
a pocket full of posies.
ashes! ashes!
we all fall away!

Into Shadow

The Higher Self is a divine mystery, an exquisite enigma waiting to be uncovered and understood, valued, and cherished; it is captivating, fluctuating, seeking to merge all the life forces, all five koshas—body, vital prana, mind, wisdom, and bliss—forever. But along the way, the self is often taught that there some of its aspects, memories, thoughts, and feelings are not acceptable. They're bad and should be shut away in the absence of light.

What some call darkness in this way is simply that which one has not yet seen or known or has not yet been allowed into conscious awareness. The ego self doesn't yet know that no part of it is wrong, awful, or never to be the object of shame. Opening poses too much risk. It's stuck, wanting to hide away some of its parts, even its strengths and virtuous ones, hoping that they'll stay hidden away once and for all, just as it had learned to do long ago to comply and be loved by others more powerful than it.

In many spiritual and psychological traditions, particularly those of Jungian theory, this phenomenon is referred to as *shadow*—the emotional and cognitive blind spot kept hidden. Shadow is the unconscious aspects of our personality that clash with our ego's ideal of self, causing ego to resist it and project it in alternative ways. This kind of resistance creates an ongoing conflict within, robbing us of our energy, and limiting our brilliance. What we hide in our shadow can be perceived by the ego as frightening—like an ocean of immeasurable depth and danger buried in shame. But the truth is, these yet-unknown facets are neither good nor bad; they are simply hidden. Whatever we might conceal in shadow got there by the absence of conscious choice. But what comes out of it takes deliberation. What's there is neither good nor bad. Some things in there are needed, they'd be useful if we could allow ourselves to open up to them. And there are things in there we'll never need. But as things go on, the longer things stay in the shadow the more difficult becomes the task of releasing them. Bringing them into the light of day is the first step.

As we venture into our own shadow, we uncover the radiant center of our own existence mundane everyday consciousness gives way to a profound awareness of our own divine nature and the divine in all other beings.

In our ancient origins, humans had one primary goal: survival. Their minds were focused on absorbing the essential information needed to stay alive. They relied on a powerful combination of the prefrontal cortex for basic logical reasoning and the amygdala for emerging thoughts, emotions and memories to navigate dangers and extend their lives. Over the eons, as survival has demanded less of our energy, our minds have naturally evolved to seek more—becoming inquisitive, searching for knowledge, and embracing curiosity. Like a fire, the human mind consumes thought and emotion, fueling our collective evolutionary journey.

The more we nourish the flame of curiosity, the greater grows our appetite for what's unfamiliar: connecting with strangers, embracing different cultures, inhabiting new environments, and entertaining fresh ideas. When our consciousness is attuned and aligned with our soul, we naturally strive for renewal; we overcome obstacles, seize opportunity, embrace complexity and grow. Our whole being becomes more capable, more skillful, and at ease with adapting to change, overcoming obstacles: broadening the abundance of our lived experience. Being aligned with the higher intelligence yields a soulful frame of mind—a blend of enthusiasm and uneasiness spawning and integrating ever-unfolding landscapes of complex psychic dimensions for us to access at will, igniting a flurry of complex inner worlds that often confound the ego's comprehension.

We are complex and adaptable beings meant to evolve endlessly. Even so, new phenomena can disrupt and confound us, leaving us disoriented, doubting, afraid, and resisting—and longing—trying to turn back the clock to simpler times. In the short term, resistance tactics may work, but in the long run, they rarely do. Old ways of being will fade away as our soul guides us to a new reality.

Think of Alice in Lewis Carroll's *Alice's Adventures in Wonderland* (1865) and her journey to find liberation within herself amid the surrounding chaos. As the familiar logic of cause-and-effect crumbles, she is thrust into a world where rules shift unpredictably. At first, she resists, trying to impose order, but as exhaustion sets in, she surrenders—not to the madness, but to a deeper truth: the only way out is through. Turning to her curiosity and intuition, she discovers an inner strength that allows her to navigate Wonderland's absurdities with newfound confidence. In the end, by her own grace, she emerges from the confusion—not just escaping Wonderland, but awakening transformed, at peace with herself.

The story begins with White Rabbit appearing to her, muttering, "Oh dear! Oh dear! I shall be too late!"

Intrigued, Alice follows him down a rabbit hole into Wonderland, where she's entangled in a maze of contradictions between her learned rational ideals and the chaotic truth of the world around her. She faced a hero's quest to survive dangers and escape her antagonists: the Mad Hatter's answerless riddle, the irascible Queen's fatal threats, Cheshire Cat's challenges to her sanity, the King's self-serving subjective rules of justice, and An antagonizing Caterpillar repeatedly mocks her, questioning her identity with a taunting, "Who are you?"—forcing Alice to confront her own sense of self amid Wonderland's disorienting chaos.

An accepting Alice adapts to it all. When it became clear that her learned rules of cause and effect were failing her, and exhaustion loomed, Alice let go of how things *ought* to be and embraced Wonderland's chaos—not as her truth, but as the reality of those in control. Turning to her curiosity and intuition, she discovered her ability to rise above the turmoil and face each crisis with resilience. Through her own grace, she freed herself from Wonderland's oppression, awakening safe at home—at peace and newly confident in who she had become.

What Suffering Serves

Suffering served the mythical Alice, as it does each of us by inspiring us to find a pathway to our higher states of grace. Suffering is a kind of wake-up call to embark on what may unfold as a sacred journey of the soul's growth and evolution. But, suffering alone is not the point. Suffering is only needed to get our attention and hold it until we consciously engage with it as a means to the learning our soul is wanting. In this light, even our darkest moments are not just times of despair but invitations to deepen our understanding and elevate our spiritual being.

In our core, every human being is in possession of courage. Like suffering, courage is not an end in itself. It's a quality that serves a righteous purpose: It is a means to wanting and finding our way to elevated states of grace. It is a means for the successful completion of the sacred journey of our soul's growth and evolution.

Knowing brings solace. Longing for grace through purposeful suffering and courage are threads that have been woven into the rich tapestry of our nature. They are for guiding us to a credible understanding of ourselves and for securing our place in the grander scheme of the universe.

The hero within each of us has come into this realm expecting suffering, ready to courageously meet it with the right measures of acceptance, patience, and resolve. The hero within us embraces it, knowing there is purpose for awakening and inspiring the self to complete necessary healing. The hero is well acquainted with the pitfalls of jumping out of pain too soon or staying in it for too long—maneuvers that would ensure its return and increase its potency. The hero stays the course.

Like the mythical Sisyphus heaving the boulder back up to the same mountaintop only to have it, again, succumb to gravity and tumble back down, an effort he is doomed to repeat for eternity, we attach to our suffering fatigue and hopelessness. Like Sisyphus, the unawakened self can be enmeshed with victim or martyr ways of being in the world, stuck in self-inflicted excess suffering. However, when that illusion is let go and suffering is embraced as a necessary, but temporary event, as an impermanent passage for the higher sake of healing and learning, wisdom happens. In other words, we cease to identify with our pain, we learn, and we move on. In this way our suffering becomes less frequent, its pain less acute. It no longer torments us. Realizing that we're more than our life travails and misfortunes, we become one with the Great.

To know that every experience—no matter how excruciating—holds within it an invitation, even a blessing, for awakening to our soul's truth is to understand the profound purpose of being alive. In our darkest moments, when grief and heartache crash into us like waves, these adversities become powerful agents of change, for shattering the old ways that no longer serve us. The pain we feel is not meant to break us, but to break us open showing us new ways to see, to grow, to transcend the ordinary. The heroic journey is about transforming our suffering into wisdom, embracing vulnerability as strength. For when we are willing to be broken, we realize that we cannot be shattered—only reshaped into something stronger and more resilient.

Summoning New Courage

In relentless pursuit of unveiling our untapped potential, the hero within all of us awaits ready to engage with our most extreme challenges. That is what happened with Donna, a devoted mom, when she faced extreme circumstances that would radically change her and the rest of her life. A self-declared "wallflower"—timid, trying hard to blend in and live up to others' expectations—Donna hit a crisis that would flip her world upside down when she discovered that her autistic daughter from a former marriage, by age 15 had been suffering sexual abuse for more than two years by her current husband. These atrocities were so heinous that he eventually would receive a prison sentence of 140 years. In her statement to the court, Donna wrote:

> *How can language begin to express the impact of something so devious, malicious, and vile that it causes a soul to shake, a heart to stop feeling, and a mind to be debilitated by doubt, shame, guilt, anxiety, and depression? Writing this impact statement has taken a year and countless drafts. It never occurred to me before I discovered that something of this magnitude could*

happen to my family in my own home. How do you put into words something that when you say it out loud, your voice shakes? How do you describe the fear, anxiety, and sense of helplessness that comes from this?

By then Donna had embraced the reality of acceptance. Motivated by her righteous anger, she would quickly move beyond any victimization and into the reality of responsibility, where she would embrace her role as protector of her child and advocate for justice. Abandoning any reluctance to act, erasing any fear, the shock aroused in Donna unforeseen bravery, clarity, and determination.

I was filled with rage. I felt betrayed. I was just livid. All of that surfaced in a nanosecond. As for the rage, I never experienced anything like that. I can see how people snap, cross that line, and kill. Yet there was logic overriding the primal desire to take him out, an overriding need to protect and take care of my daughter and handle the investigation. It came down to the protection of the kids and wanting to make sure that justice was served.

She experienced a seismic transformation, a mind enlivened by courage and clarity, that years later remains firmly rooted.

The person I was before was driven by looking good and measuring success by the house, the gardens, the materialism. Looking back, I really didn't like myself. I didn't have self-love. But if you would have asked me then, I wouldn't have said that everything's great.

I saw this as being my fault. I felt guilty, guilt and shame that I didn't protect my daughter. After everything was taken away, I had no job. I had no house and no finances. At that point, I simply had to be with myself.

When we choose to be with our experience, not to try to overpower, run, or hide from it, we allow ourselves a renewed reality that comes by pure presence and fully engaging oneself in finding our own authentic way of connecting to the Great. Though shocked, Donna responded in the absolute pursuit of justice, with love, and by grace in support of her daughter's wellbeing. A newfound sense of empowerment had taken root.

Later, as part of her own recovery and quest for meaning in what had happened, aided by plant medicines, she opened to a whole new inner world. Referring to the role of plant medicines Donna explained their benefits in her growth,

> They moved ego out of the way and created my experience of connecting to God... We can become so caught up in our head from all the programming that we received since we were born; it undoes that and helps us move the trauma.

With her new perspective, she found meaning in her suffering, using it as a foundation for expanding her consciousness and deepening her wisdom. The more she reflected on her experiences, the more she uncovered and understood the enduring truths they held. She shared a few of them with me.

> Suffering is grace. I signed up for this; it is for my soul's growth. By being within those spaces and having proof of things that happened in my life, I know it's not just faith; it's an experience, it's known, and I know at the core that there is God. We do circle back; we are energy that is not destroyed. Everything truly does happen for a reason, and it is a blessing.

That Feeling Inside

Mari's story is an inspiring testament to the human capacity for strength and resilience. Overcoming the loss of beloved family members with whom she was inextricably connected, dealing with financial and medical challenges, and upheaval of her home and school life, all of which happened within a short time, just before she reached her eighteenth birthday. We spoke one summer afternoon, when she openly shared with me her life-altering experiences and how she had responded to them.

Her childhood was an abundant mix of love and adversity. Mari's parents were married for a few years before she was born, and they spent three years together as a family. Mari's life took a turn when her father unexpectedly passed away. With her mother battling multiple sclerosis for over a decade, they relied on the support of family to help her mother continue her professional career and navigate life as a single parent.

At age three Mari was raised by what she called her "collective parents" — mother, aging maternal grandparents, and her great aunt, Dot. The more we spoke, the more it became apparent that her gratitude for their love and care helped her develop her formidable sense of self and inner strength.

Together, the family enjoyed a house in the city and one at the beach. They always made time for dinner together, with plenty of laughter and conversation. All the while her mother's symptoms worsened. Watching her mother continue to lose her mobility was never easy, but Mari always knew there was plenty of love around her. And despite their challenges, each family member remained optimistic and grateful, particularly her mother. Mari admiringly recalled her poise.

> She never complained. I've always known her to be happy, positive, and joyful no matter what was happening around her. She has an internal peace and kindness that shines through. She's resilient, and I aspire to be like her. I always have.

By the time she reached middle school, Mari's homelife, as she had known it, started to unravel. The summer before Mari started high school, her beloved grandpa, whom she regarded as her father figure, was diagnosed with terminal cancer.

> *Every single day of that summer, I accompanied him to his radiation treatment. Seeing him in that state was really challenging. But I also felt compelled to be there for him because he had done so much for us. I didn't know it then, but that would be my last summer with him. He passed away that October. He had beaten the cancer, but his body was vulnerable, and he caught pneumonia. That was a huge loss for our family.*
>
> *By then, my mother was fully disabled and needed a lot of support just to move, bathe, and get dressed, so I began supporting her. My grandma was also getting older, and so was my Aunt Dot. They didn't drive, so I made runs to the convenience stores by bus and took on work around the house. I was 14 years old, learning how to take care of people I loved while watching them grow older. It was a big shift from them taking care of me to me taking care of them.*

Under the burden of managing increasingly outsized responsibilities at home, Mari became more and more withdrawn, anxious, and despondent.

> *I felt incredibly sad. I was without my grandpa, who supported me so much. I struggled and became a little rebellious. Always a straight-A student, I started getting Cs and Bs. I had a tough time socially, too. Instead of participating in extracurricular activities like I used to, I tried to get home as quickly as possible. Before then, I did ballet, peer mediating, cheerleading, and even mentoring, but in my ninth-grade year, I decided to put down all of it. I felt lonely at school. I was isolated.*
>
> *I was also scared, really scared because I had lost my grandpa. I thought that if I helped more, I could help them each live longer. I started to try to help as much as I could because I*

wanted them to be safe, and I didn't want the others I loved to go anywhere the way my grandpa did. I always wanted to get back home to check on them. To make sure they were still there.

Amid life's fiercest storms, we can often feel as if we're untethered, lost amid confusion swirling in disbelief. Yet, even in these moments, our soul is quietly shaping a new reality, gently urging us to embrace change, find a new voice, and resonate with a higher frequency, guiding us toward renewal. However, much like Alice lost in Wonderland, our ego clings to familiar ways of escape. The true key lies in recognizing our disorientation and choosing to release the struggle of understanding, surrendering to what is.

We can become distressed when captivated by the negative spin of threat. The ego's fixation on the tangible—on matter and facts—can dull our ability to connect with our soul's deeper vibrations. We've been under this illusion for so long that we've mistaken it for the only reality. Throughout our lives, we've been conditioned to believe that we must control and direct our way back to the familiar, but in doing so, we only spiral further away from our ultimate truth.

At first, Mari chose to vigorously defend herself against any more loss and heartache. She was determined to make things right, even if it meant bargaining with inevitabilities. Soon after the loss of her grandpa, and then only a teenager, Mari took on more caregiving responsibilities. She served as de facto head of household for her mother and her grandmother. It was a lot for her to shoulder.

No one asked me to do all that. I did it myself because I was living scared after I lost my grandpa. I thought that if I helped enough, they would live longer. I didn't want [my mother and aunt] to go away like my grandpa did. I didn't have a community. I didn't have many friends. I was isolated. I had so much fear and anxiety. I don't know who I was bargaining with, but I was still bargaining, trying to be the perfect caretaker at home.

My aunt told me that I thought I was God and could make everything happen as if I was. Although that was sometimes a positive thing, for being ambitious and achieving a favorable test score or getting accolades at work, it's also a double-edged sword because it led me to believe that if I didn't do a particular something, then a bad thing would happen. It didn't allow me to rest or to relinquish myself to any kind of experience of flow that comes by my faith in God.

To go beyond familiar ordinary ways and into foreign terrain of our soul's prodigious powerful way, takes more than determination. It takes a leap of faith. At the crossroads we face two choices: a) stay alert to the utterances of our soul and surrender to its innate guidance; or b) hold on to an illusion that we—that is, our ego—will steer the ship, never mind the turbulence. Mari was at the juncture.

She accepted an invitation from one of her mom's sorority sisters to take a trip with members of her church group to visit colleges they might attend. Her "yes" opened her to a community of new friends and the opportunity to join their Bible studies group. For Mari, now 16, things were on an upswing.

The more that I was introduced to God, the more interested I became in my religion and what I believed in. I hadn't prayed before. Now, I started to pray. I was praying for my mom and my grandma, praying for them to be saved. Although I still had a bit of fear, it was less than before. I also joined the school debate team, Future Business Leaders of America, and Mentors, Inc., and completed a model UN trip. I now had friends. At home, everyone is stable. They're fine. I'm still helping after school, but I'm balancing things.

At eighteen, she would move from her family home in Washington, D.C. to begin a new life as a student at Temple University in Philadelphia where, as she recalled, "I had a ball."

But, not for long. During her sophomore year, she received alarming news of her Aunt Dot's passing. Mari credits her supportive friends with helping her cope with the grief of losing yet another loved one. She would soon graduate from Temple and attend Johns Hopkins University to earn her master's degree in education.

Back home, her grandma, now 89, had been handling much of the caretaking responsibilities for Mari's mother, which, at her advanced age, was taking a considerable toll. So, Mari, now 23, returned to D.C. and moved into an apartment nearby. In addition to the demands of her studies and a full-time job, she took on primary caregiver responsibilities for the two remaining most important people in her life. At a stage in life when most people are adapting to the challenges of adulthood, Mari was managing immense pressure juggling such responsibilities that most adults would never face. A short time later, after multiple surgeries, her grandmother too passed away, the pandemic struck, and Mari, in her own words, had "hit rock bottom." Looking back, she came to understand the deeper transformation taking place in how she reacted to loss by resistance.

> *My grandma was so important to me. I felt very alone in the world, vulnerable, afraid, and anxious. I felt I needed to control everything. I began to bargain again because I feared losing my mom, too. Imagine a dog shaking in the corner of a kennel because it's terrified of everyone and everything. That was me.*

Within each of us lies a deep well of childhood memories, where our inner children remain alive and full of energy, yearning for recognition and healing, calling for affection, care, and protection. Profound healing comes when we acknowledge them, offering comfort and understanding they may have never known. As we reclaim the parts of ourselves that once felt lost or abandoned, new vitality emerges.

We each have unique versions of children hurting within us. Crying to be heard, and known, they can grow large and tormenting. In so many ways they might show up as whiny imps, or as irascible tyrants colluding and intimidating, to get attention. They might take on bigger-than-life size demons frightening us into believing that they'll stop at nothing to get their way—fighting, shouting, ignoring, ridiculing, running, hiding. But none of these strategies work; they only create more separation. Their actions are simply attempts to gain our attention in the only ways that they've learned. Ultimately, the hurting parts of ourselves are yearning for our love and connection. To bring lasting peace to our lives, we need to bravely stand, look upon our children as lost parts of ourselves desperate for the attention and connection they've been denied their entire lives, understand, forgive, and integrate them, knowing that wholeness ushers in peace.

Mari was craving nurturing for her own young self, caught in a suffocating hold of power to control her own life and the lives of those she deeply loved, doing everything in her capacity to protect them from harm or misfortune. On top of her caregiving roles, the pain of losing another of her loved ones would be too much. At another level, it was as if unseen forces were conspiring for her to surrender, to journey beyond and find a new way of being. Despite daunting uncertainties, she pressed onward, fueled by a rising inner determination to confront, head-on, her deepest fears.

I couldn't sleep. I'd have panic attacks. I was depressed. I had lost a lot of weight. Every single strand of hair on my head fell out—gone. It just came out in clumps in the shower. I was crying every day. Sometimes, I would sleep on the floor in

> *my mom's room because I was so scared that something would happen to us at night. I was terrified. I was in an awful place. I had compounded stress, anxiety, and unhealthy patterns of thought. Although I hadn't turned away from my faith, I wasn't as active.*

It was at these kinds of moments when she was feeling isolated, alone, and in doubt that Mari began understanding what was happening to her—that she was nearing a tipping point, an imminent moment of profound transformation. Mari was about to surrender to an unchartered direction by means she had not anticipated.

> *There was one particular night when I couldn't sleep. I was stressed and didn't know what to do. I had tried medication for anxiety, meditation, therapy, and yoga all at once—none of it worked. But I had a Bible app on my phone and there I found a sleep meditation. That night, I went to sleep like that [snaps her fingers] and rested the whole night. The speaker spoke about fear. How lies are whispered to us to make us afraid, and how none of those things are real or true. God's promises are what is true.*
>
> *From then, every night at bedtime, I began reading my Bible or using the Bible app. I also joined a church here in Philly with my mom. Almost instantaneously, my depression and anxiety washed away. My hair began growing back (I have a full fro now!). I was happier. I was seeing friends again. I had felt hopeless, and now I had hope and faith again. I started to pray about many things and to give my worries away. The most important thing is that I let go of a notion I'd had since childhood, that I had to be in control. It was the old way of bargaining, as if I had an illusion of power. Everything I was experiencing, all the dark nights of the soul, was me hitting that darkest point. I think all that was to turn my face back to God.*

> *At this time in my life now, I feel at peace and in the moment. I'm able to navigate stressful moments. Other difficult things have come up, but how I navigate them is entirely different. I say a prayer. I give it to God, and then I'm like, 'All right. Well, I'll do what I can, and that's all I can do. And that's okay.' I now know that I have the Holy Spirit in me, and I can trust my instincts. That feeling inside me is God. It is always ready to navigate us if we will listen."*

The soul seeks harmony with the ego as its reliable working partner for bridging the inner world of Spirit to relationships and all other worldly areas of living. The ego does not have the wherewithal to chart the direction of our true path, that's the exclusive domain of the soul. But the good ego can contribute its unique abilities to keep us on-point and on-task and attending to our needs. The soul is imperishable, the ego exists because of the soul—it is a phenomenon of the soul with a sacred purpose of dutifully serving it well. Those of us who are seeking to know and are willing to open ourselves to the timeless truth, even if we don't exactly know how, will realize the peace of surrender. We are each being called to ascend suffering that exhausts us. We begin, as Mari did, by releasing the soul's longing and inviting divine help.

The Call

Mari's life had become a cycle of exhaustion, chasing control and prevention, yet feeling an inner emptiness that those could not fill. Her suffering, she realized, stemmed from the ego's need to control, always striving for more, while her soul called for peace. The ego, she came to understand, was to be a servant of the soul, to support her own higher purpose. Yet it had taken over, and this misalignment drained her. Despite her tenacity and generosity behind her many hard-won accomplishments, she sensed a deeper truth emerging from within—her soul, untouched by the chaos, was quietly waiting for her to surrender to it.

One day, Mari decided to surrender. She became ready to not need all the answers, just the willingness to trust her soul's guidance. Bit by bit, she let go of the need for control, of her constant striving. In that surrender, she found the peace she had been seeking. Transcending the grip of a desperate ego her suffering eased as she allowed her soul to lead.

In her act of surrender, Mari discovered true freedom. Her journey became one of trusting the soul's wisdom, knowing that her ego, when aligned with the soul, could serve her highest good.

Like a vine nurturing growth, soul bends relentlessly toward the Great. Soul, insistent on its divine perfection, vitalizes us in the here and now, and stores infinite wisdom. Just as Mari did, answering the call of soul, means attuning to its utterance of longing, and surrendering to its flow by grace.

Grace, like a quiet but potent current, feeds the vine of our soul's longing, reaching us through the subtle yet powerful channels of rhythm, melody, and harmony. We can feel its vibrations by our body's sensations, by the stirrings of our dreams, the flashes of inspiration, and most profoundly, by our emotions. As Mari discovered, grace is the very condition of surrender that we need to open ourselves beyond our ego's control and enter peace through alignment with the soul. As we listen for this, we begin knowing and trusting the soul's voice, allowing grace to lead us toward the deeper truths that nourish and transform us.

Love and learning happen naturally, but not accidentally. Just as a diamond is forged under immense pressure, so too do we undergo stages of refinement to ultimately evolve into resilient and powerful high-vibration beings. Rather than regarding life's challenges as annoying or troubling interruptions to what we *really* want out of life, seeking to learn from each of them evolves and enriches the soul's wisdom. For this, death itself becomes our great ally.

When we remain aware of the inevitability of our death and surrender, when we embrace our suffering with self-compassion, and draw wisdom from what it means for us, we bring forth a sense of completeness to our human experience. That we may find meaning in life even when confronted with a hopeless situation or with a fate that cannot be changed, we bear witness to the uniquely human potential at its best—the commitment to transforming one's tragedy into a triumph, that is, as Viktor Frankl said, "When we are no longer able to change a situation... we are challenged to change ourselves." In this way, we are alchemists capable of blending the finality of the events of our existence into another next new beginning. The old ways wither and die so that we can find a new way forward, aware that all our life will die and all that will endure is the wisdom we gleaned from our experiences.

Down Under
in me down under
bell rings, fades away,
now all hears All.

Courage to Immerse

Pain of wounds past are callings inward to uncover brilliance today for eternity. Born into a state of perceived separateness has inflicted upon each person a ceaseless unrest, an ebbing and flowing state of wistfulness and melancholy. It is to awaken, and to arouse connection to, its source, the Great. A call might come sudden and by shock. Sometimes, though, it comes as effortless as a whisper, or a gentle nudge.

Salamanca is an ancient town in the west of Spain, in Castilla León. The University of Salamanca, founded in 1218, is one of the oldest universities in Europe. Its impressive Plateresque architecture, especially its ornate façades, is a hallmark of Salamanca's rich academic and artistic heritage.

In the ancient streets of Salamanca as a young child, Maria, felt the gentle whisper of a call, drawing her attention to something far beyond the ordinary rhythms of daily life. Though she could not fully understand its significance at the time, it would plant the seeds of curiosity and longing within her, setting her on a path of discovery shaping her for a journey in years to come.

Years later as she stood on the brink of adulthood, Maria sensed a deeper purpose beckoning her—an invitation to embark on a journey of self-discovery and exploration. She would summon the courage to leave behind the familiar streets of Salamanca and embark on a journey across the Atlantic to the United States. What began as a leap of faith soon unfolded into a decades-long odyssey of profound self-discovery and enlightenment.

In the vibrant tapestry of the northwest U.S. and the Mexican Caribbean, Maria encountered both adversity and opportunity, navigating the depths of her own soul as she traversed the new landscapes and cultures. Through trials and triumphs, she unearthed layers of strength and resilience she never knew she possessed, emerging from each challenge with a deeper understanding of herself and the world around her.

Inspired by her own budding transformation, Maria felt a stirring within her—a calling to share her newfound wisdom with others and to make a positive impact on society. With unwavering determination, she dedicated herself to illuminating the path of inner growth, recognizing its potential to radiate outward and uplift communities far and wide.

Maria's story is a testament to the profound interconnectedness of humanity—a reminder that everyone's journey is intricately woven into the fabric of the collective human experience; what lies in confusion is seeking elegant simplicity. Through her courage, resilience, and unwavering commitment to growth, Maria's story serves as a beacon of light, illuminating the way forward for all who seek to embrace their own journey of self-discovery and transformation.

Years later, it was a bright fall day in Colorado when we met for our conversation. She had just completed a day working as a diversity, equity, and inclusion leadership consultant and coach. Her eyes lit up as she described herself as a free thinker who has cultivated a spiritual life that has become of great importance to her. As Maria shared her story with me, I witnessed obvious signs of the traces of a journey that had transcended the person she was before she began it—inspiring hope and igniting change in her own life in the hearts of others along her path.

I asked her about her choice to leave Spain and move to the U.S. at age 24, alone, with little money or proficiency in English. She explained that very early in her life, she had a compelling realization of her Spirit that she innately trusted. The call was so persuasive that it stayed with her even after twenty years, reminding her of the inner certainty that pushed her to embark on her journey in the first place. In her words:

> *I remember becoming aware of Spirit at different moments in my life. The first came when I was four or five. I had a clear realization that we don't die. At the time, I didn't know where it came from, and I was excited. So, I hurried to our kitchen to share the good news with my mom: 'You see, even if we get a knife stuck in us, and we get really hurt, we don't die!' I knew then that we may die in our human form, but our Spirit does not. I knew that Spirit is both something one believes in and something that one feels; it will be with you throughout all of your journeys and your entire existence here on Earth. By it, we don't die.*

Longing is the soul's call to lead the self out of confusion. This was true for Maria, who, despite adversity—or perhaps because of it—persisted onto her true path.

Attuning to Soul

When lost alone in a forest, most people will become anxious and aimlessly walk in circles wasting their precious life energy. But a longstanding guideline of outdoor safety says: stop, calm, rest, collect your focus, get your bearings, and then move on gradually, or find a safe place where others will spot you and wait for help to arrive.

In moments of our lives when we're lost, most of us push on determined, ignore warning signs—of obstacles or pain—waste our life energy and losing when self-reliance mightily fails us. Because our journey here is to awaken from the density that has swathed our light, we don't have time to walk around lost in circles looking outside for the next cure.

We're all here to embrace and love ourselves without apology and find our way to our own inner light. Our refuge is reached in going deeper within to our true selves cherishing who we are as we are, unabashed, unreserved, and gracious. This is our sacred priority.

Awakening is birthed through stillness. As when lost in the forest, the idea is to calm and surrender to where we are. Right answers then have clearance to show up. Finally, we will discover a path towards inner peace through new ways that will emerge, naturally—from deferring to others to trusting our own intuition, from stubborn perseverance to contemplation, from disdain to kindness, from reproach to forgiveness, and from self-hatred to self-acceptance.

We each possess vast reservoirs of wisdom. Every experience we have is like a skin that's being shed, to reveal the majesty of our soul. Every emotion we have can inform our soul's navigation to the Great within us.

Maria's journey of self-discovery reveals the profound transformation that unfolds when one answers the call of spirit with deliberation. She would eventually accept her soul's invitation to journey inward, explore and embrace her authenticity. Her story teaches us that we will lose our way many times: that it is in getting lost that our most important work begins.

At the age of 15, I began to question if there was more to life than just going to restaurants and hanging out with friends, as enjoyable as it was. Then at 18, I met an older man who introduced me to the writings of American anthropologist, Carlos Castaneda. Through his books, I discovered an entirely new perspective on reality—one that dove deeper into our intrinsic being and the energy that connects us all. This was definitely outside mainstream thought at the time, but it spoke directly to my soul's yearning for something far greater and compelling.

This ended up being my initiation into a new way of seeing life and of seeing myself. From there, so much of my life began making sense in a way that I had felt intuitively. I began to know that there was something else within me, and within all of life, present at a much deeper level than meets the eye! Up to then I could sense it, but I couldn't quite put my finger on it. Now I could. I became excited about my growing certainty that there is more.

But Maria's navigation to her path of new possibilities would have its challenges. A sudden family crisis abruptly thrust her into a different direction.

Around that same time, I started to go through a very difficult period with my family. So much betrayal and deception that had been covered up for years abruptly became uncovered. So much of it was inconceivable. Now, knowing the truth led us to realize that so much of what we had been living was a lie, including how we were situated financially, and especially about the foundation of our family. It was very shocking.

Maria chose to move away from the chaos and angst of her family situation and search for a radically different lifestyle and way of being. It began with a summer of wanderings and connecting with friends on Spain's southern coast. A move in the right direction, her travels, though, stirred up a longing within her for something much more. As she reflected:

> *I enjoyed the way that I was living but felt as if something essential was missing. Certainly, there was freedom, but there was not the devotional aspect that I craved to dedicate my Higher Self to. So I knew that I could not live like that forever.*

At 24, Maria's yearning for more inspired her to venture to the Ramtha School of Enlightenment in the U.S. Pacific Northwest. Ramtha's lessons encouraged and supported her to delve into her core inquiries around the nature of human life and the relevance of one's personal identity. The model of learning was experiential. Immerse and learn. Reflection. Action. Repeat. She took on big topics ranging from human nature, and ultimate purpose, concepts of morality and immorality, the concept of the soul, mortality and vitality, our connections with others, applied neuroscience, and the intricacies of space, time, and existence. Committing to rigorous training while sustaining a living was difficult enough but navigating daily life while managing her legal status in the U.S. layered on more.

> *A point came when I questioned if—by leaving Spain and going to the U.S.—I had done the right thing. I didn't speak the language. I tried to enroll in college courses but needed a visa to do so. I realized how few options I had. There was a lot of stress because I had to save money to attend the Ramtha school. I also had to leave and return to the U.S. every three months to maintain my legal status. I then found that I couldn't continue*

traveling. On top of it all, I had a romantic fallout that added more pressure. I fell into a deep state of depression a loss of identity.

I felt as if I had lost my connection to Spirit completely. I had entered a dark night of the soul. I didn't know what was happening to me. I had never experienced anything like it. Each day I woke up seemed dark and heavy. I felt confused and alone. I was very confused.

Now, looking back, I see clearly what had been happening. I was experiencing a very radical change, moving apart from my family and from Spain to a faraway, different place and culture. At the same time, I was learning a new philosophy and way to see the world that deeply contrasted with my Catholic upbringing. Adapting to it all had placed great physical and mental demands on me. Compared to my family life growing up in Spain, I was never without anything I needed; I always had it all. Living alone in the U.S., there were severe issues that I was facing from not being able to legally work including fear of getting caught and deported. However, I was dedicated to pursuing spiritual teachings. So, for me, getting deported was the absolute worst thing that could happen.

Through a series of distinct yet intersecting disruptions, Maria eventually gained insight into how her childhood had shaped her to experience those specific difficulties. She explained, "As a child, I rarely felt seen for who I was. I grew up in invisibility. I felt like a zero on the left side of the decimal point. I simply did not count."

Abandoning those tired ideas and useless attitudes handed down to her while growing up, she reignited her commitment to her spiritual path. She mustered the boldness to ask her friends and healers for assistance. That alone was a bold step into a new stance of her claiming self-confidence.

After facing my inner demons and with some help from an iridologist, I eventually came out of my depression. I felt as if I was being born again. I didn't recognize myself. I felt more open, loving and light. My life force returned and I was ready to face the world.

During that dark night of the soul, I now know that my ego was paralyzed for a purpose—it was so I could integrate my new experiences, knowledge, and the changes I had made. I could not have integrated them all without being depressed because my ego would have questioned and resisted it all. It was, in a way, as if my ego was knocked down, shattered, so that I could see all my negative patterns in full view. Then, I responded to them and began integrating the new knowledge into my brain.

Things began radically shifting. Maria was absorbing lessons of resiliency through experience and continuous self-refection, evolving into a more complex, accommodating level of consciousness, deepening her inner wisdom, and learning to live in a state of grace.

I decided to take some time away from the school and traveled to Mexico to visit friends there. Many things started to line up differently in ways that made clear the power I held within myself. That I can create my reality—I came to believe as absolutely true. I create my reality! Of course, I think it's easier to say that you create your own reality when you create great things, as opposed to when you create shitty things [laughs]. I realized how everything I had learned at the school about manifesting was entirely true.

The culmination of Maria's challenges and her successful negotiation of them, especially in the light of so many critical variables, along with her commitment to relentless self-reflection gave rise to a whole new level of being for her, especially as she relates now to the inevitability of experiencing pain by living attuned to her emotions and giving them expression.

> It takes a lot of energy to suppress these emotions hoping to avoid feeling their inevitable pain. But I know now that when in pain, if I don't turn and go toward it, if I resist it and suppress what needs to be known, I am wasting my valuable life energy. As emotional pain gets activated, if I go into and through to the other side of the pain, any need to push and exhaust myself is released. I have learned that there is darkness we must venture through to reach light.

Maria trusts that she has a reliable connection to Spirit to inform and guide her. She knows the connection is not always straight-lined. Whenever she veers off, because of her courage and her resourcefulness honed by real world praxis, she finds her way by opening to what is.

> It varies from day to day. Most of the time, I feel closely connected to my Higher Self, and sometimes I'm not so much. When that happens, I feel a sense of loss, disconnected. It's then that I make a choice to do what I know brings me back— meditation, yoga, time to reflect, and quiet time in nature— and helps me go into and through and grow from whatever pain I'm experiencing.

Maria's quest is a reminder that our longings from the soul are invitations to enter mystery, to complete lessons, and to stay alert for more will come. Longing is the soul's guiding inward, to quiet depths to embrace weaknesses, level imbalances, and settle unrest to align the self with the true Self and bring to light our own unique kind of wholeness.

Maria's story of authentic self-emergence serves as a reminder that regardless of the inevitability of challenges and uncertainties upon every path we take, we are never truly alone. Soul and Spirit are always present, gently nudging us onto our true path. By attuning to their subtle signals, and responding compassionately, renewal and self-discovery now come to her naturally. This fundamental trust in life, of accepting adversity, invites meaning, purpose, flow, and joy to her life.

The Return

Historian and philosopher of science Thomas S. Kuhn, renowned for reshaping how we understand scientific and social change, gave lasting voice to the concept of the "paradigm shift". He suggested that a crisis once underway is the necessary force needed for any great change in our thinking, in our being, in nature itself. As it is with extreme events in the natural world, crises that we human beings face, large or small, are the essential forces driving essential change in our lives. The challenges of our being, as they unfold and become increasingly evident, are not to be absolutely feared and thwarted. As Kuhn wrote, "And once we understand nature's transformative powers, we see that it is our powerful ally, not a force to be feared or subdued."

Even though a volcano may appear to erupt out of nowhere geologists have revealed that underneath the surface—beneath layers of soil and rock—an accumulation of Earth's inner energies shifting over time has created an intensely powerful core that will ultimately blast into a fierce explosion. Volcanos benefit Earth and humankind. According to the U.S. Geological Survey:

"Volcanic materials ultimately break down and weather to form some of the most fertile soils on Earth, cultivation of which has produced abundant food and fostered civilizations."

Like a volcanic eruption, we can become shaken into upheaval by unexpected shock or loss, but these setbacks can leave us with previously unknown ways of being and becoming wiser.

Many of us have encountered extraordinary moments of discovery that led to radically new ways of being, some frightening, even stunning. At such times, if we choose to move toward the upset with curiosity, we're more likely to find a new truth and more resolute purpose.

Often this is the work of the soul seeking access to its own essence, deploying its means for reaching learning it needs, whether subtle or sudden. Accidents, tragedies, disasters, losses, and illnesses can spiritually awaken us as José experienced by being comatose for thirteen days after his biking accident. From it he was propelled into a genuine bond with his Self and the Great.

José had gone through the agony of physical and mental recovery after his bike accident, but something else was stirring inside him. His core beliefs about himself and his purpose in life were shaken. It had been a frightening and painful journey for him and his loved ones, but it had also led him to newfound clarity, depth, and resilience. He noticed that with each passing minute, fear was replaced by a connection to something greater than his previous self. When José surrendered to this unexpected transformation, he felt a renewed presence and complete confidence in the Great.

We don't think much about our day-to-day lives because we're so busy thinking about the future. You spend your life thinking about what if—but what life really is about is that you are here, now. You cannot control what's going to come. Whatever comes is supposed to come, and that's okay. This is true regardless of whether you believe it or not, or even if you think you can anticipate and be completely prepared, ready to handle whatever might come at any time. ... For me, it's a big thing, knowing that I'm not as powerful as I had thought myself to be. What's amazing is that I now feel a sense of freedom. I feel that I am being taken care of, and no matter what happens, divine grace will take care of me.

As there are opposing, complimentary forces asserting among us—yin and yang, negative and positive, masculine and feminine, turmoil and peace, love and fear, what is hidden by dark and illuminated by light—there dwells within each of us a mysterious way vying for love to overcomes strife. Often, there are no clear choices in this great paradox of life and death—in our cycles of life, death, rebirth and renewal, even so at the level of the soul. There is only our ability to grasp that these are not opposing but complimentary forces; two faces of the one undivided whole, both necessary, neither dominant. Each in service of our transformation. The soul is an alchemist endlessly seeking to integrate all the forces. By the merging of opposing powers, the soul ascends the illusion of duality, purifies itself of any residue of resistance, to contribute its uniqueness and become one with the Great Source.

Dullness is to be still in the mundane of the status quo. Healing is magic evoked by the fever of suffering—the medicinal call of the soul to alleviate another hurting want of an ancient burden. We are alchemists when we embrace and allow suffering to transform what's ill-fitting and create new life in consciousness. Consciousness expanding is to create life into wisdom of your soul.

As the self grows wiser, more attuned to the soul's longing, more astute to the true nature and presence of Spirit, then catastrophes—thunderbolts and shock waves—become less. Softer, subtle ques are all that are needed to awaken.

Like light rain, a precipitating event might gently come carrying messages. That was true for José, who, shared with me an episode that happened one quiet night while in his recovery, in and out of a comatose state when he was alone in his hospital room. He awakened briefly to a moment of lucidity. Just then he received a message. He never knew for certain who spoke it. His best guess was a female hospital staff member, whom he never saw again.

She came into my room and told me, 'This injury is going to help you be in the present because that's going to help your recovery—to be in the present.' She emphasized: 'Not in the past, or the future but, the present.' I do clearly remember what she said. I also remember that I paused, looked at her, and wondered, What the heck is she talking about? Why is she saying that? That doesn't make any sense. In time I came to believe that was a message I truly needed to know, and to keep. And so, after these years, I have. Although I don't remember who she was, I do remember what she said.

Regardless of how they come, the purpose of precipitating events is to summon our attention to a fertile moment. Coming in the right measure and precise timing, they are an invitation to experience a different way of being. They are heralds for announcing that an old way is reaching a natural end of its useful life, and now is a good time to release and move beyond and into the new. The ease and fluidity with which one navigates these transitions hinges upon a willingness to listen and welcome what it might lead to.

Like a beam of light passing through a crystal prism, qualities of our own being, across each of our five layers, are revealed to us as we do the work and ascend to higher levels of self-love. Expanding our consciousness by bonding with our soul allows us to break free from limiting beliefs and discover the intricate layers of our true selves: That which is our nature comes to be revealed. Growing means embracing all aspects of our being, no matter how fractured or hidden they may seem. This requires careful listening and allowing, but eventually, the right experiences will find their way to us.

Deep within each of us lay hidden wellsprings, currents of divine love that stir; these are tributaries of our essence aiming to flow untamed. But along the journey, by our ego fearing their potential and unknown depths, we've dammed them. Yet deep down, our soul yearns for something different.

José's relationship with the Divine shifted dramatically from the limited beliefs of his past to one grounded in his true self. He explains,

> [The accident and recovery] brought me back to reconsidering the whole notion of my relationship with what I consider to be God. I had believed that as human beings, we considered love to be conditional, a trade-off. I had believed that God would take care of me if I was good and did the right things. Of course, I also wanted God to like me, so I tried to be pleasing. That's an old way of believing that I learned from my parents as a child.

As altruistic and caring as he was before the events—which is apparent from his having achieved a doctorate in education and his lifelong work in support of people at the margins of society—by relying on the loving relationship that his wife and he have co-created, this traumatic experience opened him to even greater compassion and compelled him to action. He has volunteered over 700 hours of his time in healthcare settings, bridging language and culture gaps among healthcare providers, and patients with brain injuries, and their families. He strives to foster understanding and promote optimal physical and emotional healing for all involved. José's kindness runs deep, and his sincere commitment to serving others is unwavering. For instance, as he shared, "I feel that not giving back would be a very selfish thing to do—not sharing all those beautiful and wonderful things that came to me."

As we spoke, I wondered what other surprising things were waiting to be revealed to José. He'd come to understand more dimensions of life and death and trust and fear, but with so many more mysteries out there, he seemed open and ready.

I was struck by the glaring synchronicity across many important domains of José's life that have come to fruition on his road to recovery. A U.S. citizen, he too is a first-language Spanish speaker, who surmounted barriers to higher education, who had already been working professionally to open access to healthcare across cultural and linguistic barriers. Then, upon his accident, with the persistence and skill of his wife, Iris, José also had to navigate healthcare access. It seems as if the inner workings of his soul landed him into an ever-deepening expression of empathy.

Understanding the perspectives of others is a powerful way to cultivate empathy. When we embrace and celebrate individual and cultural differences, and willingly open ourselves to vulnerability, we tap into the divine essence that is present in all of us. When the innate curiosity energy of Vijnanamaya, our wisdom sheath, is activated we gain new insights and deeper understanding of ourselves, others, and the world around us.

All at Once

Hilary has an MFA in creative writing, is a published writer, has a private coaching practice, and has taught and trained others to teach the Hoffman Process. She is a mother of four and, at the time we met for this discussion, a recent grandmother to twin boys. She began our conversation by sharing conflicting outlooks she had about herself as a child.

> As a little girl, I had incredible faith. I would go out in the fields at my parents' farm in New Jersey, having this relationship with nature that felt wondrous and magical. At the same time, I felt something terrible was always about to happen, something that I could not handle. I was paralyzed by anxiety, anxious about people in my family dying. I've always had both things: Feeling that life was good, and that a benevolent graceful force was looking out for me, and also feeling as if it wasn't.

Hilary would face three traumatic events involving two of her closest family members. Happily married with four young children, living an idyllic life in New England near her parents, everyone was healthy and prospering—until things would change abruptly.

Her father, athletic and in robust health, was diagnosed with an irregular heartbeat. A routine medical procedure went drastically awry, resulting in progressive brain damage. While in recovery, he re-invested his retirement savings, unwisely losing everything he and his wife had.

> *My dad started to know what was happening to him. So, out of concern for the family and himself, he starved himself to death. It was a 10-day process that was beautiful and the right thing to do. I was with him when he died. It was quite beautiful and, yes, extremely sad to lose him. But it was a total fucking miracle. Up to this time, he had not made any sense at all. Yet, before he did this, while I was crying next to him at dinner one night, holding hands with him, he patted my hand, and said, 'Don't worry, nature has a way of taking care of things if you let it.' It was so lucid. I believed him. Then, he figured out a way to die. I knew in the moment he said that, that he was right, and I knew in my soul, there was going to be a miracle. I had just lived through a miracle of [my child's] recovery, and I knew what it felt like.*

Around that time, Hilary also witnessed her youngest child, a toddler, being hit by a car, resulting in a severe head injury; her daughter couldn't speak or open her eyes for fifty-six hours and recovery would require treatment over the following year.

> *When [my child] was hit by a car, my body intuitively knew how to be with her body, I am not sure I saved her life. I am sure I was surprised by how calm and present my body stayed. I am sure that I provided her attuned and regulated presence.*

Whether that had any impact on her survival is not provable. The miracle for me was that I could count on myself in a way that I didn't know I could and count on life, on grace, to save my child.

I've always had the practice of praying and a relationship with God. On the drive to the hospital from where she was airlifted, I got the kids in prayer. I got us all to pray out loud for her. It was an hour-and-10-minute drive, and during that prayer session, we were all praying and crying out loud, begging God to save her. I had a crystal-clear moment of knowing she was going to be okay and telling everybody that, as vivid and as clear as if it were a fact.

That was the same thing that happened when my dad said, 'Don't worry; nature has a way of working things out. If you let it.' I knew he'd be okay then, too. It's almost like the sky parted and Light came down with some glorious music, as if it were a movie. I'd enter a state of grace, stay there for about ten minutes, and then realize how things were: 'Wait a second! He doesn't have any money, he's losing his mind!' or 'Wait a second, she's in a coma. What the fuck?! This is not okay!' I couldn't sustain the faith in the face of such scary information."

A third such event also involved Hilary's daughter, who, as a young adult, was drugged, abducted, and reported missing in Germany for sixteen hours. News would eventually get to Hilary and her husband that their daughter had been found, hospitalized with a brain bleed, after being brutally raped and left to die.

This was bad. I was shaking like a leaf. I don't know if I had a moment of faith. I don't think I did it until she was found. But I did not go hysterical at any of those times—never.

As a child I had a story that I was a little hothouse flower wimp—it was a deficit thing—that I was a little spoiled brat, that I never had any hardship, a little White privileged girl that had never been tested.

Ultimately, what I learned is that I can handle life. I handled all three things. All three worked out. In other words, rather than reinforce my anxiety, these traumas reinforced my faith. I'm realizing I really can count on myself to have my own back, and I can count on myself to show up in a disaster. I do think I'm a very powerful being. I've never been this high in my connection to Spirit. I know that I can count on myself. When teaching at Hoffman, for example. It doesn't even seem to be coming from me, it feels like it's Spirit coming through me. I know how to get out of the way. And that's fine because we don't have to plan any of this.

Rather than reinforce my anxiety, these traumas reinforced my faith. But it's because they worked out — the person who was supposed to die died, and the person who was supposed to live lived. Strangely, these things brought me closer to feelings of safety than ones of tragedy. [There were] significant traumas, and there were miracles. From then on, I began to believe in miracles.

I don't know all the machinations of it, but my belief is that before we incarnate, we plan with God, like what we're going down to Earth school to learn. I don't know how much of a hand we have in actually setting up the events, but it may be quite a lot. I don't fully know. Life is a mystery.

At pivotal times in our lives the vitality of fire energy, new waves of awareness might crest within us, bringing sudden emergence of insights and understandings that challenge our existing worldview. This can feel destabilizing, akin to being swept away by powerful currents. We may fear losing our sense of control or our identity in the face of sudden change.

Fire symbolizes inner essence ignited, the core vitality that drives us toward profound realization and transformation. It is the energy that fuels our passions, ignites our dreams, and evokes a clear signal from our soul's longing. Yet, amid the juggle and rush of daily life, we often overlook or underestimate our inner flame, catching only fleeting glimpses yet it remains perpetually seeking to intensify its brilliance. And if left hidden from our conscious awareness for too long, it will burst forth with profound clarity bringing to the surface the truths we have buried, the desires we have ignored, and the transformations we have resisted. This moment of revelation can be both awe-inspiring and unsettling, but it is always an opportunity to realign with our soul's purpose, reignite our vitality, and embrace the powerful force of our inner fire.

For Hilary, moments of startling clarity played a powerful role in awakening her sense of inner authority. By acknowledging and nurturing her inner flame, she deepened her journey of self-discovery, growth, and spiritual fulfillment. As a parent, partner, guide, and coach, she learned to translate these insights into tangible transformations—for both herself and those she supports.

Great Exceeding

The *I Ching*, an ancient Chinese oracle of change originating between the 10th and 4th centuries BCE, includes a reading for times of crisis and transition that *I Ching* scholar Steven Karcher calls "Great Exceeding": "Though the structure of things is in danger of collapse, there is a creative purpose at work in the breakdown. If your situation does not nourish you, if it will not support new growth, push it over and leave. Let the strong force gathering in the center penetrate and move you. This can be a very important time."

The stories of Maria, Donna, Hilary, Mari, and José reveal individuals who, when faced with extreme challenges, responded by drawing on their higher energies within—courage, determination, grace, compassion, and resourcefulness. Each of them also embodied deep humility, which opened the door to acceptance and meaningful inner change. These shifts, though born of hardship, became sources of lasting strength and transformation in their lives.

José turned toward his life-threatening experience not with resistance, but with acceptance, presence, and trust. Rather than hardening, he softened—cultivating a deeper self-compassion that allowed him to witness his own wounds without judgment. In doing so, he reshaped his understanding of himself and of the Divine. What emerged was a more grounded, intimate relationship with the Great—a relationship no longer rooted in fear or striving, but in reverence, authenticity, and quiet belonging. From within Hilary rose a formidable new strength shaped by the challenges she had faced emboldened by her commitment to guiding both herself and those she loved through times of great crisis. She traversed layers of fear, anxiety, and self-doubt, and on the other side found courage, compassion, and presence. Long accustomed to dimming her own light, Donna awakened the benevolent warrior within. No longer shrinking, she met ruthless injustice with fierce, grounded love shaped not by anger, but by purpose. Her protective energy became a shield for others and illuminated ways for them to rise.

The term, *dark night of the soul*, originated in Spain: (la noche oscura del alma) and is attributed to the 16th-century Spanish mystic and Catholic poet, St. John of the Cross; it refers to a phase of passive purification in the mystical development of the individual's spirit. From an early awakening in childhood, Maria navigated storms of life—family crises, cultural upheaval, financial hardship, questioning purpose, and ascended her dark night of the soul. From her early youth, she held fast to a deep inner knowing, later guiding herself through the vicissitudes of a hero's quest. She now stands with unshakable conviction in the truth that her eternal Spirit lives within her—and with it, the knowing of how to return to its light and to reveal it in the lives of others. Mari endured deep exhaustion and made profound personal sacrifices—aiding her loved ones through serious illness and at their passing. These adversities provoked her to experience a dark night of the soul. Yet in that, arduous, shadowed place, she opened to a deeper wisdom and emerged with a steady sense of joy and peace—enduring, carried gently within her.

The extraordinary responses of these five people underscore the power of embracing what might appear incomprehensible. A deeper truth is revealed when we recognize and embrace that the soul's growth often emerges from times of discomfort and uncertainty, even in the most extreme circumstances. More truth comes as we realize that the soul's longing speaks at the precise volume required for us to hear it and meets us at the depth our experience requires.

Among many insights, their stories teach us that by living from a place of grace, we unlock previously unknown personal capacities to face adversity, pain, and the struggles of suffering as invitations to emerge into the authentic Self. Their stories also reveal the suddenness of transformation—moments that pierce through the veil of routine, startling the ego and revealing the superior transformative fire within. These moments, like sudden bursts of heat, have the capacity to stir a person's depths, drawing attention to their true nature. To the unaided eye, these profound glimpses of the soul's creative energy are rare, transient, and elusive passing as swiftly as a swallow in flight. What may seem like an unfortunate crisis is, for those ready for awakening, a profound opportunity, though such moments might easily slip from conscious awareness if we are not attuned to them. In this way, crises become a surge of longing from the soul to reveal what is within.

Receiving the soul's longing, whether it comes in a gentle flow or a powerful surge, requires more than merely hoping or wishing for it. It is about actively and deliberately tuning into it, allowing the current it sends to connect with the whole self, like light flowing through an ocean's depths. Living this way, in cadence with the soul, ends the illusion of separation. It is connecting to the great Self within. It is loving the self in the way of the soul.

Chapter Nine
What Heroes Know

A hero knows that they must be vigilant in discovery: mindful that the purposefulness of living is for grasping the way of their soul. They live their lives guided by this that becomes their true purpose: the course rarely linear, at times wandering sometimes doubtful, still they stay true to knowing it. The hero understands faith: that searching for purpose is to be living on purpose. Every day they revolt against the restrictions remaining open and ready knowing that their innate brilliance will emerge in its own way. Nothing is forced. Being heroic means reminding oneself that their life is intended to serve a unique purpose even when its purpose is unclear. Heroes know that awakening is constant and may at times appear to be in direct opposition to one's needs as a living, breathing physical being. They focus on a higher order and balance this tension between matter and ethereal.

Purpose is not dependent upon words to be understood: the hero knows it by heart. Sometimes the hero even feels they have always known it. Then life becomes elegant. At other times it can be as if the hero is caught in a whirlwind of confusion, disorientation, self-doubt, second-guessing, and helplessness. Even so, the hero ventures on, seeking and following their longing as best they can. They sense its vibrations and search for subtle signals. They hope to one day know and rest in their knowing, informed by the wisdom of their lived experience that complacency is dangerous. Until then, they know that engaging in strategies, striving to figure things out, and fixing them in the logical ways, would be in vain and only would yield strife. So, the hero saves their precious vitality remembering that what matters most is to stay trusting in their capacity to listen, to receive, and to interpret the endless stream of vibrations carrying pure intuition for keeping on the true way—their own unique, spontaneous truths flow directly from the secret teacher within.

A caterpillar's metamorphosis is a heroic feat. It begins life as a voracious eater, but when the time is right, it abandons its appetite and seeks quiet refuge. Hidden inside its chrysalis, the caterpillar dissolves, liquefying its old body, leaving behind only the most essential tissues. Its remaining cells follow an innate blueprint, a biological *imago*, to rebuild itself into something entirely new. Piece by piece, wings, antennae, eyes, and a long proboscis from its head take shape in perfect harmony. From the outside, it may seem like nothing is happening, but inside, nature is orchestrating a masterful rebirth. Just before it emerges, the chrysalis even begins to hint at the butterfly's colors. Then, in a final act of transformation, the butterfly breaks free, pumps life into its new wings, and takes flight, forever leaving behind its crawling past.

By relentlessly listening for the quiet voice within, fulfilling the destiny of their soul, a hero embodies the essences of curiosity, courage, resilience, and self-forgiveness to dissolve and reform their lived experiences into a new way of being. A hero replaces old worn narratives of failure and self-doubting with lessons of grounded hope. They live in the present, revealing the ever-evolving version of who they truly are, informed by where they've come from as they are emerging into an expansive, accommodating new reality. No longer restrained by vicissitudes of slyness and deception or by the guise of shame, they embrace the durability of kindness, compassion, mercy, and love—new ways of informing their outlook and guiding their actions. The heroic way is to continuously break free from old habitual ways of *looking* at the world to truly *see* the world as it is. They embrace transformation freely and live in the present, soaking in the brilliance and wonder of who they are and merging as one with the natural order of life. And most importantly, the hero stays open to learning through trial, error, and candid self-reflection: they know that without staying awake and abiding by the longing of their soul's path, they might well be seduced by the lesser energies of the old ways. The hero has learned that the longing of their soul leads to certain required journeys, by sacred calamities that might, at times, seem endless. Without inherent trust, every calamity may well devolve into catastrophe, and the hero knows they must remain alert to their life in all its dimensions: as suffering nears its end, grace arrives.

Soul's Descent

The hero does not dwell in imagination. They know that life on Earth demands work, although it is of a different kind. It is as the French alpinist, René Daumal, referred to in his treatise, *Mount Analogue*:

> *You cannot stay on the summit forever; you have to come down again. So why bother in the first place? Just this: What is above knows what is below, but what is below does not know what is above. One climbs, one sees. One descends, one sees no longer, but one has seen. There is an art of conducting oneself in the lower regions by the memory of what one saw higher up. When one can no longer see, one can at least still know.*

At some point, the soul will call the hero to venture into the abyss to rescue abandoned lost parts of the self, to claim and integrate them so as to form a more balanced, wiser, whole self. The hero stays attuned for the call, by attuning to their soul's longing ready to move inward and to be guided into the higher regions of Self. The hero continuously engages in these sacred cycles of descension, immersion, ascension, reflection, learning, and living. The hero becomes an expert in this. This is to live imbued with purpose.

***

To experience moving with such intention, I invite you in this moment to relax your gaze, take a few full, deep breaths. Then turn your attention to inward, to your soul. Ask your soul to show you an opening, a certain doorway that opens you to being completely kind to yourself. Allow the image of whatever comes to you and allow yourself to be drawn toward it. Let your soul guide you to that doorway. Curious, you follow towards the doorway and step through it. You begin feeling your way along a winding staircase, its steps are seemingly endless. As you safely are guided to descend, take in the spaciousness surrounding you. Follow the stairs until they fade into a void below. Step by step, continuing downward until there are no more stairs. There at the bottom you sense the presence of a reassuring being that you intimately know.

Moving toward that reassuring being you can sense gentle, loving vibrations emanating from their kind heart. Looking closer you notice that this being is also afraid. Intuitively you understand them. You see that they are quite young. And that they are delicate, though worn down by burdens of doubting, distrusting, and living with a lot of uncertainty. You understand that they have been overwhelmed by having been disregarded, excluded, and at times, even made to feel ashamed of who they are. Deprived of love, fearing more abandonment they have learned to shrink and hide. They have at times acted out by resentment and irritability. It could be easy to label them as malicious or unruly. But this part of you simply craves empathy, acknowledgment, and affection. It wants to belong.

This is the young part of you that has survived by siphoning life from within you, trapping and choking off emotions from their true expression. This underworld part of you has learned to survive by manipulating and deceiving others, and yourself. They learned to do this to stay safe from harm. This frightened one was trapped long ago by a lie of unlovability that you believed to be true about yourself. Left alone and unhealed, this will continue distracting you from your true essence and leading you astray from your life purpose. They are hoping that you will understand how they learned to become as they are: that you will accept and love them for who they are.

This is a yearning of innocence crying out to be acknowledged and loved by you. They will continue their stirring until given full appreciation and recognition that they deserve for enduring so much pain. Their suffering summons a journey for you into an exact kind of healing—to claim this, and all parts of yourself—by taking the time to seek out, find, and love each of them by greeting them with tenderness, and embracing them wholeheartedly into your whole Self. This is a sacred quest of your soul.

Pricked and Stung

Once cast in the recessed shadows of her own psyche, then illuminated by courage, the hero steps into the lucidity of her own beam of sunlight, revisioning herself, reflected in a mirror of truth rendered by a heart of loving kindness, held with compassion, and fed by appreciation for who she is becoming. She anticipates that the old, learned ways that had trapped and fractured the luster of her essence will eventually come to an end. She will keep them as long as she needs them to learn. Embracing the duality of the old memories, she had once rejected, with new vitality the hero completes her quest to wholeness. The castaway fragments of her life till then, rather than discarded become precarious shards of a shattered mirror that once reflected a life rife with pain and suffering, now re-form as diamond essences of wisdom by her life transformed. The hero becomes whole by living as her soul intended. All heroes' journeys end by embracing human contradictions, reconciling, and integrating them all in the formation of a more perfect whole.

The journey of every hero ultimately ends, but the ending isn't about finality: each ending marks the start of something new. The hero's journey follows a cyclical path, where the end is simply the transition to a new chapter—a return to existence with newfound knowledge and power within the Self that the hero shares with the world around them.

To know a hero is to know the Higher Self within. A hero lives authentically, courageously facing challenges worthy of herself, all in, wholly committed, actively and deliberately attuning to what she needs to align and merge with her Spirit. She becomes greater, by divine measure, in proportion to her willingness to become small in ego of self, to humble and enter her void within. The hero becomes adept at that sort of loss so that she may sharpen her skills and rid herself of that which no longer serves her.

At times of crisis, the hero momentarily allows herself to become weak. She patiently loses the old ways so that she will replenish herself with new truths seeking their way to find home within her. About the time when she thinks that she might be falling apart at the seams, peels back the veil and finds that there's irony at play—that her suffering is loaded with noble purpose. Ralph Waldo Emerson spoke to this cycle: "Our strength grows out of our weakness. The indignation which arms itself with secret forces does not awaken until we are pricked and stung and sorely assailed." And skillfully, the hero invites in the pain of her suffering unabated.

Sacred Calamity

A sacred calamity is an orchestrated dilemma—carefully arranged by the quiet teacher within—inviting us to turn inward, confront what holds us back, and free ourselves. A calamity shakes us up, evokes our curiosity, and grabs our attention for mastering yet another lesson to add to our sacred chest of wisdom. A sacred calamity is an invitation to transform.

Among the several lessons that we can take away from the five stories previously told, is that such extraordinary moments hold enormous potential for re-envisioning ourselves and how we approach living. When we recast those tremors, that at first shock and frighten, as invitations to ascend they take on an entirely different dimension. Certainly, there's no benefit to trying to get around our reactions; however, great value is created by stepping into a calamitous event with complete presence, and with above all, curiosity. As each of us is a hero of our own life, we may choose to move into all of our experiences with a sense of exploration. When we do, we truly see, and we grasp the truth of our existence.

We've all had, and will continue to have, our own kinds of sacred calamities: by the death of a loved one, a life-threatening injury to our child, extreme risk to our health or capabilities, abuse and betrayal by someone we trusted, destruction to our homes by fire, by flood, or extreme weather. At first, they might seem like random misfortunes, incomprehensible dilemmas, no-win situations, and disastrous losses. At times we cope by blaming ourselves, other people, circumstances, or simply trying to write it off as bad luck. If awakened at the level of Vijnanamaya, our wisdom sheath, we grasp the possibility of a higher purpose at play. We can see that what had been causing us so much consternation might also be the budding of something intrinsic to our becoming happier, freer, or more loving. At first it might not look that way but, as the years unfold and upon deeper reflection, their value to us can become clear. It's then that we become humbler, more accepting, and at peace.

As the stories of the five people show us, there's a way of experiencing what on the surface appears only catastrophic that what renders them sacred is our response to them: accepting all of whatever has come to us, expressing honestly, opening ourselves to ourselves with vulnerability, reflecting for the wisdom that's available to us, and ultimately choosing to live on with a more tender, and courageous, heart. We become our own hero worthy of our deepest respect, unconditional love, and admiration. When all is said and done, there can be no hero without sacred calamity and a calamity without a hero is just an awful experience.

***

Within each of us is our diamond essence untouched by the past—a rare and precious gift—radiating compassion and grace. It is real and it is tangible. Although, sometimes out of fear the uneducated ego resists and hides from it. But, even in our dark moments of doubt, its light beckons us toward the certainty of hope to be renewed.

Embracing your innocence is to reclaim your wonder. We are asked to trust in unseen guiding forces even when what's ahead is obscured by shadows of the past. Consider taking this moment to heed the call of your inner light and embrace the hope eternal within you. Be open and receptive to whatever may come to you. For in that sacred space of vulnerability and openness, you may rediscover greater resilience for navigating your life. Take a few deep full breaths to quiet your mind. Allow yourself to be present at the spaces between each breath as you read to yourself the words below as you envision your Spirit radiating within you, there in the center of your chest, your Anahata, the holding space of love within you.

My own essence is pure loving innocence. It is always reminding me of the many important memories I hold deep within my heart. I choose with courage and grace to step into the unknown within myself. In this moment, I hear my Spirit calling softly, reassuring me. It is my guide. In this moment I allow myself to be enveloped by the presence of my loving Spirit. I open to its gentle whisper coming to me like a feather freely dancing on a gentle breeze.

Pause a moment to open yourself to whatever way you experience your Spirit's presence. It might come as warmth of a flame, flickering light, or as a gentle caress of a breeze whispering through space within you. Feel the ease, as you embrace it. Surrender yourself to this peaceful way of being with yourself. Let ease and wellbeing wash over you, the soothing power of your Spirit grounding you in the present. In this connection, present to yourself, feel the peace in simply being. See the beauty in simply being as you are.

Embrace the love emanating from within yourself; its vibrations fill your body. With an open heart—joyfully smiling or painfully wincing, shedding tears, or taking deep breaths—welcome the truth of who you are. You are beautiful and you are love.

Open yourself in this moment to any messages that may be coming to you. Welcome them with warmth and openness. The deeper your connection, the greater is your wisdom and joy. The connection to your own Spirit is made manifest by an inseparable bond. Its light is yours and can never be extinguished; it seeks to strengthen and grow its presence as you follow and attend to its call. Its call is the call of your soul. Connecting to your Spirit brings a deeper and more profound respect for what it means to be human holding your important place as a member of all humanity—sharing and loving this existence.

Chapter Ten

By Love's Way

While learning to love ourselves might be the greatest single lifetime challenge that any of us will encounter, it is, hands down, the greatest gift of our lifetime. The rest is mere window dressing. Self-love is the rain that feeds our river's flow. It is the key to unlocking the mystery of who we truly are, the window to our happiness thrown open, the treasure of our self-gratification, self-appreciation, contentment, and all other joys that come by being fully alive. By it, we thrive. It is within you, there in your heart space, waiting for you to freely open to it anytime that you wish.

Falling in love with yourself doesn't mean that all your problems will evaporate, and you'll not know struggle. It does mean that how you face your struggles radically changes. Though challenging, the act of self-love can become simple. We want self-love: we thrive on it. Our self-lovingness blossoms when we stop trying to prove that we're lovable and we discover that we already are: that we surrender to what is our true nature. Self-love begins with knowing that we are already enough, as we are right now. Not one of us needs to do anything to earn our own love. There's no need to remake who we are. There is no need to strive for status, money, or approval. Right now, in this moment, each of us is deserving of our own love. Nothing is more vital to our self and our soul.

However, over decades, much of humanity has followed a misguided belief that self-love indicates narcissism, self-aggrandizement, self-pity, and frailty. In my work over twenty-four years providing leadership, life and spiritual coaching, facilitating adult transformation retreats, and working for diversity, belonging, and inclusion, I've found that most people, to varying degrees, carry the common misconception that self-love implies weakness. Yet, I have also witnessed, and have experienced, the potent, exhilarating, and sustained, force of self-love taking root in many of those same people, and in myself.

As children, we learned to turn away from loving ourselves. For the sake of survival, protection, and family sustenance, we unconsciously learned to block our love energy. This alienated us from our true core. But now we can find our way back.

Speaker, author, and teacher, Regina Louise, who from birth suffered repeated wounding of rejection by her parents and after enduring more than thirty foster homes by age eighteen, refers to the courage it takes to love oneself and the potency of joy it brings:

"Unconditional love permits me to know what is true about me: I am right to be here! I am right to love myself! By grace alone, I am worthy."

The great quest of all is to embrace the self without reserve, courageously, willfully, calmly, and completely. There is no more extraordinary gift we can give or receive than to live fully and with purpose—to intentionally love ourselves. Nothing is more essential or worthy of our time here.

Being in love is our natural state. We long for it. It is for us to open to. In loving ourselves, we become our own hero, embracing the thrilling adventure of living freely. By choosing to vanquish the hold of shame and guilt, we unlock our heart's window and welcome love into our being. Although it might take a great deal of courage, what could be more deserving for us to enjoy?

***

You can feel your way into your own love spark. It dwells within you moving as waves of light, like liquified particles. It is loving energy, given off by the soul and concentrated in the space of the heart, Anahata. We can reach it through conscious intention. Begin simply and gradually, quietly opening to any sensations present within the space of your heart. It always helps to have a mindset of patience and to be in a space of quiet calm.

Watch the flow of your breath—each inhale and exhale. Notice your breath going in, the space between, and your breath as it goes out. You are being present to yourself in this moment. What do you notice as you inhale? As you exhale? At the still space between your breaths, what do notice?

Listen closely. Feel the sensations coming to you. Our longing and love often whisper through the body or move gently, like a leaf drifting upon a breeze floating across the inner skyscape of our mind. This, your longing, is calling you inward to find your unlimited love. Your love and your longing are inseparable. They come from your soul. They are one and the same, the pure nature of the soul that is within you. You might feel it as stillness. Again and again, practice finding love and longing within your heart space. Invite in the unique sensation of your longing, your call to love. Allow your body to sense it and through your sensations you will know it.

In practicing this way of being, you are allowing the natural rhythm of your breathing to show you to your longing. The more you listen with your body and notice what comes softly within the space between your breaths—the more you will come to know it.

***

We each carry wellsprings, currents of divine love that stir tributaries of our essence to be flows untamed. Consider spending this moment placing your attention on the flow of your breath. Begin by drawing two or three deep breaths and pausing between each one. Place your hands heel to heel, or simply one hand palm facing inward, at the front and center of your chest, upon your heart space, your Anahata. As you breathe, ask your soul to guide you to a space within you where the light is dim. See in front of you what resembles an entrance to an undiscovered cave. Step closer, up to its entrance. Patiently, look around.

Now, holding a candle lit by the light of your soul's loving presence, take a small step in and look around. Get a feel for this space. This cave is a safe space, a space to take shelter from any need to prove, or to need to know, or any expectations. In this natural place you are simply being. As you do you grow curiouser and curiouser. The more that you look around this shelter, the more familiar it feels. You have a felt sense of it too. You are curious and want to explore this safe space within. You are taking a moment now to simply be.

Natural shafts of light begin to glimmer in your cave. One shaft of the light draws your attention. As you move closer to it, you feel at ease and at home; you feel peaceful. This is an intriguing place. You venture further, guided by light. You find among the walls of your cave ancient markings, rock etchings that portray parts of your past—petroglyphs of your life, images that evoke memories that are important to you. They are of memories that hold emotions that have not been expressed. They are as if parts of you have been trapped in time and the only way to free them is to understand and appreciate them, now, by a new light.

Seeking to know you might ask: What are the emotions here? What am I fearing? Which part of me keeps them hidden away? Why have I been needing to know, or express, from this memory?

Answers may come to you in words, by sensations in your body, or by other, wordless ways of knowing. If any doubt or a need to avoid arises, simply acknowledge that they have and continue opening. Open yourself to your own answers.

Take a deep breath and continue asking yourself more questions like these: "Where in my body do I hold expressions that I've yet to feel and set free?" Patiently listen. Receive whatever comes. There is a treasure trove of emotions—some are unknown, and some are frightening, some enlivening and some lovely—all are awaiting release. Ask your soul to help you to understand them all so they can come to life and be freed. Every emotional memory is an archive that we can draw on for knowing and evolving our love wisdom.

Each time you ask for the emotional truth you open yourself to your internal power of expression. Each time you allow answers to surface, acknowledge doubt, but aren't deterred from your truth, you heal yourself and expand the vitality of your soul. Whenever you commit to setting free any trapped emotions, one by one, you are breathing life force, prana, here and now.

Once again turning to your soul, you might ask, "Where in my body do I keep expressions trapped?" Trust that clear answers will come. Wait and consider what does, feel it, accept it. Ask for any one of those feelings to come up so that you can feel it and release it in this moment. Go to it and breathe into it.

Soul Power

By the sacred journey of self-discovery and liberation, self forges a relationship with the soul, of expansion and inner wisdom. With each released emotion, the bond becomes more robust: it is building karmic soul power too, paving the way for profound transformation freeing from the shackles of the past and stepping into a brighter, existence within our eternal center of higher consciousness. This is to create a different order of reality that encompasses extraordinary well-being, profound peace, tranquility, serenity, and cosmic unity.

You are a whole beautiful being of complexity fully deserving to be loved and respected. No part of you is unworthy, unacceptable, immoral, or flawed. Even among the vilest acting, it's the vile that's the problem, not the Being. Look upon any parts of yourself that you have wanted to disown, abandon, or hide away in shame. All of them have been craving to be known for their intention and regarded with respect. Reach out an open hand of acceptance and offer a warm embrace. Welcome them in from the shadows. There are simply all parts of being yearning to rejoin all other parts and become one whole being of love.

All of us came here, in our lifetimes, to become a seamless, whole, fully integrated, powerful being, alive and merged with Spirit. As it is, all people are completely worthy of love, as each is now. Finding the love inside is rarely a one-and-done event. It's iterative. It requires practice, repetition, and skill.

***

Where within you do you feel fatigued? Patiently, as if in a dream, make your way up to your pain. Pause there. Show yourself kindness. Admire yourself, your courage. Tap into your willingness to move beyond fear or discomfort. Approach the place of your distress. What's there?

You may come to a wounded place that you've known for a long time now, or a newer one, might be coming to mind. The hurt that you feel from it holds an ache that won't abate, a heaviness you can't seem to get out from under. It might sometimes leave you languished. At times it can be a real beast. Restless and intimidating. You've tried to tame it. You run; it follows. You cry; it quells and returns. You name it; it morphs. Talking about it only seems to make it more real. You dread it. It seems immune to treatment. There seems to be no way to make peace. You carry it with you wherever you go. It has been with you your entire life. Sometimes, it seems it will never go away. Yet here you are on its doorstep. Tenaciously, you are facing it. Steadfast. Brave.

Imagine that you have been endowed with perfect insight — you are holding within your hands an animated glass ball containing your entire life up to now. Contained within it is a composite of everything you have ever experienced, felt, and thought. With perfect clarity you can see and know all that's within it. Hold it directly up to your mind's eye and look closely. What's happening? How are you feeling about it? What part of you might need to be seen, understood? What does this part of you need from you? What's the pain that it carries? What would bring it relief? Pause a moment to receive answers.

As you might grow curiouser, ask it more. It's been there to serve some purpose. What is the wisdom it holds? What is the most important message you want it to know? What needs to happen from here on? Listen, then take a moment to tell it what it needs to know from you.

Reassure yourself that there is nothing wrong or bad, or that anything is broken or needs to be fixed. Nothing is wrong with you now, nor has there ever been. Speak kind words to yourself. Again, pause. How does it feel to speak kindly to yourself? What happens when you do? Do you accept your kindness? Or do you push it away? What happens when you do?

Whatever pain you carry comes from what you have been taught or told to believe about yourself. Any edgy, harsh, gloomy, unsettling, or scary feelings, any discomfort or illness that you harbor is the result of unexpressed emotions trapped within you, waiting to be brought into the light of your awareness. They are not you.

Pain subsides as love transcends the artificial limits that we possess. Author, bell hooks, shares wisdom she has gained on the challenges of loving oneself:

> *Only love can heal the wounds of the past. However, the intensity of our woundedness often leads to a closing of the heart, making it impossible for us to give or receive the love we are gifted. To open our hearts more fully to love's power and*

grace, we must dare to acknowledge how little we know of love in both theory and practice. We must face the confusion and disappointment that much of what we were taught about the nature of love makes no sense when applied to daily life.

Venturing to the higher realms of the self loving the self and feeling bliss that flows from it, as pleasing a notion it is, can be disorienting and frightening. But to evolve into the higher realms uncertainties about life and self must be faced with open eyes. As sure as we might commit to opening ourselves to the powerful unknown, our ego will resist. It resists because of the threat it faces by letting go of the familiar beliefs and ways of being that have served to keep it in place.

Our inner child remembers when, by their superior power, our parents invaded us; versions of them became part of us in some not-so-good ways. And it has been challenging to get them to leave and return to their places. So, we resist giving into more powerful forces regardless—life, vibrancy, curiosity, fulfillment, appreciation—that could launch us to adventures of promising new beginnings. We have that decision to make: stay skeptical and hold on to the comfort of our familiar past, with its tailings of ego sensibility, or embark on an inbound journey daring a life of absolute self-compassion.

Our Birthright

To be self-loving is absolutely our birthright. But, over our lifetimes, and due to inevitable adversities from birth onward, we grew skeptical and denied ourselves that truth. As a reminder to yourself, right now, try taking a breath, then pausing, and saying to yourself out loud: "I love you." Pause another moment. How did that feel? What did you think right after you said it? Or could you not say it at all? If a critical, skeptical inner voice came up, that's normal. We all, at times, fear even our own quiet love. In some way, each of us has learned to deny ourselves. Some more, some less, but all of us have, to some degree, learned how to be afraid of love.

Loving yourself is knowing bliss. Yearning for our joy is innate to each of us even more so than our yearning to speak, to stand upright, or to walk; its yearning is ceaseless and can never be quashed. It might occasionally become suspended in time and place, here in a body. Still, in our softer moments, when our wounds have healed and we know who we indeed are, we will know it. After all the battles are over and our wounds have healed, we will look deep within ourselves and become our most authentic selves, embrace ourselves with unconditional love, and hold ourselves in unyielding compassion. And we'll want to keep doing it.

Our blissfulness awaits within all of us: it awaits us at the very core of our being. Although it is important to recognize this, it is even more essential to learn how to access it. Though we long for the peace of bliss, sometimes it can feel like an impossible quest. That's why life places so many opportunities before us. We are learning to uncover it until we no longer need the practice.

Challenges arise from others who don't understand us, from our daunting feelings, or even from our limiting beliefs that hold us back. It's easy to believe that something must be wrong with us. There isn't. We've simply been taught a particular way of looking at life and need only find our own way to heal. Sometimes trying to get it all figured out, striving to find the causes for the effects of our feelings holds up our healing. Healing comes by simply committing to feeling and setting free what needs to be. Committing to trust in the process is essential.

As each day passes, so too do opportunities to heal; for all of us, time is coursing. At any moment we have choice—ignore these opportunities and keep them hidden, or find the courage to set them free. As it is, we are both captor and liberator. The soul wants to free the expressions, all of them. This can be done by committing to being with any emotion and all memory it brings up. It can be an uncomplicated act of self-love.

When a heart is filled with self-compassion, our wounds become our vital force of expansion. With eyes wide open amid struggle, engaged in discovery by new realities, we become stronger, wiser, more tenacious, and present to our true essence. Our pain and our fiery embrace present an opportunity to heal and evolve that we too often shy away from. To ultimately free ourselves, we must choose and turn courageously inward, to meet our suffering with the reality of acceptance, and explore its depths until what is unearthed manifests itself as wisdom and renews us.

Parker Palmer wrote that suffering could break our hearts by one of two ways. A brittle heart will be broken into shards, shattering the self while only a supple heart will hold and allows suffering to break the self open to reveal, to know deeper, and to experience many more of love's variations.

Of Loving Self

Self-love is both a way of being within and a relationship with ourselves that grants us calm, compassionate acceptance. Self-loving means being fully present to yourself, knowing that you absolutely are deserving of joy, inner peace, and bliss. You have befriended yourself. To happen it involves the commitment of zero other people; aside from the benefits others might receive from knowing another who is self-loving it involves only the one, you. Self-loving people are the kindest, most generous, and most loving people on the planet. Self-love is powerful.

Like a beam of light passing through a crystal prism, as we reach higher levels of self-love our essence becomes flawless. Expanding our consciousness by bonding with our soul allows us to break free from limiting beliefs and discover the intricate layers of our true selves. Growing means embracing all aspects of our being, no matter how fractured or hidden they may seem.

This requires careful listening and allowing, but eventually, the right experiences will find their way to us.

This notion of the immense power that comes by loving ourselves has been around since at least the 12th century, when St. Bernard of Clairvaux wrote his treatise, *De Diligando Deo* (*On Loving God*), in which he proposed that loving oneself was essential to overall wellbeing and spiritual evolution. Even so, for many of us growing up in modern times, the idea of self-love was as foreign and remote as St. Bernard of Clairvaux's claim is old.

Today there is an emerging appreciation coming into humanity's shared consciousness for self-love and comprehending its immense influence. We now know that we can intentionally cultivate ability and broaden our capacity to love ourselves. It's always a choice we must make, often several times a day. Each time that we commit to that highest vibration of love, within our most concerted domain, our self, we create sacred opportunities for personality transformation and spiritual growth. Self-love is within our grasp; evoking it is not to be complicated.

***

One simple way to evoke self-love is through praxis of the soul—a continuous cycle of deliberately learning, then applying, what's learned into tangible actions through the five realities of acceptance, responsibility, presence, active learning, and wisdom.

You can very simply create your own experience of self-love by entering into the reality of presence. Let's try it now. Begin by pausing and becoming present to yourself by taking a few full breaths. Allow your eyes to focus softly. After your vision softens, ask your soul to show you a rosebud at the center of your heart space, one with its own unique color, shape, and scent, ready to bloom. Any kind and color will do as long as it feels right to you.

Then, once you have an image, or a felt sense, of a rosebud in your heart space, place one of your hands over this tender bud and feel the warmth of your own gesture stir within you.

Imagine the bud within you is now blooming; it's opening to vivid, intensifying colors that please your eye and helps you further relax and be present to whatever is happening for you in the moment. Allow it time to show you all its features. Enjoy its aroma and its leaves as they reach to light coming from within you. Its thorns are there in such a way that it can only be touched by you, or by others with your consent. The feminine pistil within the center of your rose is receptive and yielding new growth. The masculine stamens that hold fertilizing pollen reach out and provide nourishment to the pistil. As one, the feminine and masculine aspects commingle, creating a connection within you. Feel appreciation for your rose and its gratitude to you for keeping it alive and thriving in the comfort of your heart space. Welcome the freely flowing, loving affection as your rose blooms within you.

With even more brilliance, your rose blossoms broader, fuller, and abundantly colorful until it completely fills the space of your heart with quiet comfort. You know that your rose can never die. You can return to it anytime you wish and in any way that you please. Take a deep breath and fully open your eyes. Enjoy being present to yourself with the love you created.

***

Recovering connection to the natural love within begins with a search for what was buried long ago. Try this by taking three slow, deep breaths. Start each with an inhale from the area of your tailbone and follow it upward. As breath reaches the crown of your head, hold it for a few seconds. Follow the exhale back to the area of your tailbone.

With each breath, creating space within, greeting whatever emotions arise with compassion and curiosity. Shower yourself with forgiveness, appreciation, and love. Acknowledge your full, rich spectrum of experience. Acknowledge the inherent value in who you are by simply living here, now.

Continue to breathe from your tailbone to the top of your head pause for a few seconds and release your breath.

You might need to gently remind yourself that you are whole and complete. No part of you is flawed. There have become parts of you closed, hurt, and neglected, and now trapped in fear. They are essential to embrace, integrate, and learn from. If judgment comes, don't resist, invite it. Open to it with curiosity. Acknowledge that being human, you have harbored ways to defend and keep yourself safe—when as a child you learned to hide your light to keep yourself safe. To become aware and to accept all facets of self without harsh judgment is an act of kindness vital to finding true purpose in this lifetime. We cannot discover truth by way of the false self. It's only on the path to authenticity that true life purpose is revealed.

As emotional truths are acknowledged, one bears witness to the innate dignity of living aligned with the soul. Pain is a clue to trapped expressions, fragments of the past, striving to be brought into the Light, forgiven, and forever released. By this act of transformation, the past becomes valuable. Potent choice is made to learn from, integrate, and reshape the past into novel sources of wisdom in service to your whole self and to realms beyond this place and time. It's a conscious release of untapped intrinsic value. No emotion-rich experience is to be cast aside; by loving awareness, turning to, with kindness, is to heal.

When pain from unloved, hurt, or suffering parts surface as doubt, anxiety, or fear, speak gently to them with a sincere "I love you" until it penetrates deeply. This will begin the healing process. Let this phrase become your life mantra, and then, look for the inevitable healing to follow.

Each step to healing paves the way for infinite liberation. Over time releasing trapped emotions becomes fluid, easing navigation through inner landscapes with grace and ease. Affirming love for the self, is to align with the final state of innocence our soul seeks. This, the longing from within.

Kristen Neff, Ph.D., leading author and pioneer in self-compassion research and practice, discovered that being self-compassionate in moments of suffering consists of three core components—self-kindness, choosing to be gentle with and understanding of ourselves rather than critical, harsh and judgmental; recognizing our common humanity and feeling connected with others in life, and not alienating or isolating ourselves; and, mindfulness, being fully present and aware without overreacting, exaggerating, or feeling overwhelmed, and not ignoring our pain but, simply experiencing it as it is.

***

The following offers a moment for you to go within yourself with compassion, to further heal yourself. I suggest that you allow your eyes to softly focus, or perhaps better, ask someone you trust, to read the following:

Begin by taking a full complete breath. Picture yourself standing on the edge of a vast emptiness. You peer downward, feeling a mixture of fear and fascination for the unknown depths below. But you remind yourself that fear is a sign of courage in action. Tremors running through you are echoes of past wounds, fragments of your being that have split off from your consciousness and now long to be reunited and healed.

Move into the void and find what has been discarded or hidden. Seek disparate, orphaned parts of yourself, kept from the compassionate heart of your precious being, misinterpreted, treated harshly, cast out. Commit, in this moment, to recover them and regard them as valued contributions to your inner wisdom. Search within the tearful memories of your childhood. Explore the cavernous corners of ignorance for the brilliance of your being that is shrouded by a fog of fear. Give yourself permission to have faith in your own boundless knowledge and recognize that there is no need to conceal any aspect of yourself. Embrace the parts you have learned to hide with kindness and acknowledge them as integral pieces of who you are. Feel the warm sensation of your own self-acceptance.

With an abundantly loving heart, invite your fears, as you would an innocent child; greet each of them with a warm embrace of generosity and acceptance. Assured of your infinite capacity, trusting that your heart is filled with boundless compassion, reach out to gently touch wounds you find. Without knowing better, in following the lie of unlovability you might have learned to ignore your hurts and stray from your true path. You no longer need to. At this time, acknowledge, understand, embrace, and accept all parts of you; no part of you is to be left out. Call out to the innocents within you who are hurting. Bring the castaway shards of your crystalline cells into the warmth of your loving heart. Allow all of your parts, all of your memories to be seen and embraced in the warmth of your soul. There is room for all of you there.

As you are opening to yourself in this moment, what do you see, or hear? They are eager to be understood and accepted, noticed, and expressed. Give your memories a voice to speak what has been kept frozen. Listen close. What do they ask of you? What do they need from you?

Luscious Love
Down, following, down,
into the abyss of you.
Braver, falling, knowing, discovery.
Comes no valor in aimless wasting this one precious life.

Awakening aroused holding, releasing,
uniting life-longed-for-embrace with that,
which is you,
my Luscious Love.

We are here to feel and feed upon the flow of luscious love from the liberated cells of our bodies from the lowest point of our spinal column upward, then back downward, endlessly pooling intensity in surges that could overwhelm one not ready. Lusciousness, the expansion of our innermost essence of Atman, our spiritual core invigorates the physical body, our prana with vital forces, perfecting our thoughts and infusing our emotions, elevating our wisdom, and dwelling within the eternal center of our consciousness; it is our bliss sheath.

As spiritual beings, we thrive on love. Our soul hopes we too will yearn for it and will seek it without ceasing. The body thrives on it. It cannot be earned; it is only to be opened to. Luscious love is ours to embody and hold. When we do, luscious love manifests in the matter of body and sacred unity takes place. We become a site of spiritual alchemy of ethereal and matter. As we release the old ways, we free up new, creative, authentic ways of being.

***

At this moment, consider opening further to your own loving nature. One way is to start at the tail end of your spine. Draw a full breath all the way up your spine to the crown of your head, pause, then release it fully. Follow with another full breath up to the top of your head, pause, then release it fully. Repeat this until you experience calm naturally radiating out and into your whole body. Feel calm settling within—as you breathe to the bottom, melding with the gravitational pull of Earth—and grounding you. Feel calm settling as you breathe to your top, opening to light coming from above. From the tail of your spine to the top of your head, your divine spark is seeking expansion. Let this be effortless, radiating above you and, at the same time, anchoring you from below. You're grounded by and immersed in your own Divine Light, freely radiating warmth within you. Steadying you. It is yearning to fill you up. Allow it. You are meant to feel luscious. Drop into, down below, inside, as you feel its deep bass vibrations, the low tonality within you, melting into your body, longing to be released and expand beyond your skin. Explore this. As you do, what colors come into your mind's eye — magenta, orange, amber, emerald, azure, indigo, purple? Breathe into the pulsations of luscious within you.

It is important to acknowledge that you have expended so much of your life energy in earnestness to meet the many demands of living in a body here on Earth. By nature, you deserve joy. So now, let's expand the flow of your own luscious love even more. Allow your body's own capacity for rejuvenation flow from within you freely and, by vibration, flux, and pulsation, invigorate you. Feel its vibrations welling up within you.

Place your attention on where these love vibrations are coming from. Feel your way to it. If needed, ask your soul to show the way. Your spirit guides will help too. Then place one of your hands upon that spot—you are lightly touching your wellspring within; naturally, at the same time it brings you lightness and grounds you. This is your body contributing to your evolution, fulfilling its purpose of opening to and radiating light of love to all parts of you; waves of love light beaming throughout your body, enhancing your vitality. As an orb of light, it flows effortlessly from the base of your spine, slowly, upward, along your spine, pausing, and circling the area at your waist. There, it mingles orange, marigold, and amber light. Then the orb of your light moves to the center of your chest, your Anahata, blending healing rays of emerald, jade, and sage radiate outward from your physical body to all other layers of your being.

You are both grounding yourself in your body and connecting to your Spirit—melding the physical you to Earth's gravity and the ethereal you to divine light circling you. By doing this, you seat your soul's presence firmly within you, which will guide you to your purpose in this lifetime and help you know your bliss. You are knowing your truth and manifesting your holiest desires. In this holistic state, you become open to steady streams of lusciousness, ensconced in the true purpose of your own unique being. Though incomprehensible to the logical mind, difficult to accurately capture with words, your body knows the sensation of your true self. Whenever you need to connect to your truth, you can find this place within yourself. From there, you will know what you must know to be who you must become.

Allow yourself time and listen to them closely. Call to and patiently listen for their subtle voice. You might welcome them using these words: "Come to me, little ones, into my light of compassion. I appreciate you beyond words. I know of your great tenacity, tenderness, and innocence. As I grow and heal, I will become fully aware of the grandeur of your being and love you above all else."

Take a few full breaths and bring yourself back to the present moment.

This way of opening to yourself might be new and unfamiliar, but from now on, vow to learn to love all parts of yourself. Unyieldingly accept, without condemnation, every emotion, thought, and action you have ever experienced. Without their variety and range, there would be blandness and lifelessness. The tension they've brought instills motivation to discern from and choose among what you genuinely want and need to become whole, living in joy. In reverence to yourself, bless all your experiences—of all kinds, all nature, by all intensity and variety—as sources of wisdom.

Opportunity is always available for you to tap the vein of preciousness within yourself simply—by expressing gratitude to yourself for your courage to be here and for all that you do to keep your life going—nourishing yourself with healthy food, keeping yourself safe, moving your body, playing, learning, meditating, nurturing your relationships with loved ones, and resting each night to prepare for tomorrow. Freely acknowledge the energy and time it takes to show up lovingly and caring for those close to you—your partner, kids, parents, siblings, extended family, friends, acquaintances, and colleagues at work or school. Out loud, thank yourself for the importance that you bring to all of them by simply being.

Living a good life requires attention, time, personal resources, skill, and energy. Tell yourself, in this moment, that you appreciate how much you care, work, do, and love; how you remain committed to living a valued life and leaving behind positive memories. Most importantly, recognize that by being who you are, you matter to yourself in this sacred journey that you're on.

***

Endless paths to enter the mystery of self-kindness can be simple. One way to begin is by gently releasing any tension in your shoulders and taking a deep, full breath and releasing it completely, then another or two. Feel the ease of each breath as it flows into and out of your body. Now, bring your attention to one of your hands; notice the various sensations within it— the pull of gravity on your fingers, how your hand naturally takes on a familiar shape, the sensation of air on your skin. How would you describe these sensations? Flex your fingers. Reach out and touch something, then close your eyes for a moment and find a few words to describe what you're feeling.

Now, shift your focus beyond your hand to something colorful; colors can evoke emotions. Observe what you see in the colors and notice how they make you feel. Where in your body do you feel that emotion? Identify it as a sensation and stay with it for a while. How long did it last? Could you repeat the process with another emotion?

Finally, take note of any thoughts that come into your mind—first one, then the next. Just like each heartbeat and breath, thoughts and feelings come and go.

Research has indicated that the average emotion lasts about ninety seconds before it naturally begins to fade—unless it is consciously or unconsciously prolonged. Take the emotion you're feeling now? What is it? Follow it. Where does it travel within you? Does it eventually evaporate? More than one emotion can be felt at the same time; some contradict the other, while others exist in harmony. Which ones are with you right now?

To make this more interesting, ask yourself to invoke your great Self, connected, powerful, and peaceful. Your rational mind might think it knows a better way, but here, your body does. Let it show you. Follow its internal pull to your own place of strength and peace. Where in your body is that located? Once that's clear, then place your hand tenderly on where you feel it most intensely: perhaps it's at your heart space, head, throat, stomach, or lower back?

Often, we are taught to deny these centers of power within us and defer to our rational mind. What's happening for you? Perhaps this brings you to places that have been denied, that need healing, places where you might need to be kinder and more understanding.

Again, reconnect to your great, connected, powerful, and peaceful feeling. How familiar is it? How far back in your lifetime can you recall experiencing it? Perhaps it was there in your childhood when something delighted you. To rekindle it speak to this part of yourself. Welcome it as you might a loved one. Acknowledge it as important to you.

Move closer to your own unique feelings of self-kindness. Feel compassion for yourself. Allow yourself sympathy for all the times you felt alone, uncared for, overwhelmed, grieving, or sad. Give yourself permission to feel the outflowing of self-compassion that you have. As if reassuring a child, a friend, or a loved one who is hurting, tell yourself the words you most deeply want to hear in this moment. Tell yourself now whatever it is you need to hear. Speak words of kindness to yourself. You might say something like: "I admire you for your loving heart, for your resiliency, for your search for truth, for your authenticity, for your courage, or for your curiosity." As these words sink in, offer yourself forgiveness. You might think: "I know that I have, at times, forgotten, ignored, blamed, or berated you. For those times, I am sorry, and I ask for your forgiveness." Take a moment now to pause and receive your words of compassion from yourself to yourself. Open yourself to your forgiveness. In this moment, fully breathe in your healing words.

There is never a time, an action, or a reason for which you cannot forgive yourself. To deny ourselves compassion and ignore our pain perpetuates cycles of pain. But, turning toward ourselves for the sake of healing, even if we don't know exactly what to do, if we intend to be compassionate, we graft a split of ourselves and foster regrowth. This is the natural intention of our being—to return to ourselves lovingly, repeatedly. This is to build our own karmic staying power. Each time you heal this way, you strengthen your wholeness.

Chapter Eleven

In Stillness

Stars are the most widely recognized heavenly bodies. Those such as the legendary Orion Nebula, were created from interstellar clouds of dust and gas. Ripples in these celestial nebulae cause pockets of matter to grow large enough for gravity to take over and pull it all together. As a cloud of matter collapses upon itself, the material at the center begins to heat up and create a smoldering core. From this, a protostar is born—the blazing heart of what will one day be a new star. The night sky is adorned with stars, comprising a magnificent galaxy view. Without these shining lights, our sun included, we would be in complete darkness. Like those twinkling points of luminescence, each one of us can become a star and bring brightness. The only thing standing in our way is our refusal to awaken.

Each of us, like protostars are capable of expanding far beyond our imagination. Each cell of our bodies is like a different mind, a brain with its own consciousness that urges us to listen to our own unique calling that presents to us through our three levels of vitality—the formative, the transformative, and the ethereal. Everything that we have thought, done, and become, in this lifetime and in the others before, is held within our soul. Each time we respond to our expansion, our vital energies become even more vibrant, like feeding oxygen to the fire. But we either don't believe that we have these kinds of wisdom, or we forget that we do. Regardless, every cell of our body remembers and will never stop calling out to us to listen for them. It is our responsibility to listen to our inner voices and stir our energies. As we do, we rediscover our inner truth and tap into our own boundless strength.

Every cell vibrates a conscious intention to live on your unique purpose. Each moment that you allow yourself to attune to it and be urged on by it, your life force grows more vibrant. Like oxygen to the fire, following your longing feeds aliveness, clarity, peacefulness, readiness, and naturality about yourself.

The quest to fulfill our great purpose begins with healing our wounds of birth and of childhood so we can learn from the wisdom of their scars and move on to true love that's sourced inside of us, exclusively for and by us.

Longing feeds the appetite of becoming, a hunger summoning the hunt of a life living in fulfillment of its true purpose. Longing calls to the place of inner peace within the body. From the moment of conception, within mother's womb there began attachment to physical matter.

The cleavage of birth aroused a quest to embark upon a higher journey for reclaiming and rejoining all the self, to be charted uniquely by the soul. A soul's journey is a venture inward to find and return to the bliss of oneness with the Great Source. Constant aching comes from this highest longing—the call from our core summoning us to stillness, to know it forever—and never to relent in pursuit of it. The soul guides the heroic self to live authentically and to learn the ways of returning to silence within. Silence is the domain of the soul within the self. Over time and with practice, access to its peaceful rejoining becomes as natural as breathing. It is meant to become. All beings deserve it. It patiently awaits.

***

The following is a very simple way of acknowledging your true Self and connecting to your capacity to love you as you are, and from that state of loving yourself, know your purpose in life. Stand before a mirror and press your heels and each of the opposing fingers together in front of your chest, your heart space—Anahata. Spread outward the index, middle, and ring fingers on both hands while keeping the tips of pinky fingers and thumbs touching. The heels of your hands should also be touching.

Take a deep, full breath or two, then pause and look into your eyes. As uncomfortable as that might become, hold your gaze. Each time you divert your eyes, breathe into your heart space, and return to looking into your eyes. As you gaze, also notice, in the center of your chest, what you know to be inherently true about who you are—that you are a magnificent being carrying within your body a spark of the Great.

Ask to be shown your purpose, or purposes (often we have more than one); ask to know it clearly. Vow to be open. Answers may come to you now, or later, in the form of ideas, emotions, physical sensations, synchronicity, or by some combination of these—whatever the form, know that you will understand it, if not immediately, then eventually. You might also ask to be open and aware when it's coming.

Strong winds from storms release topsoil from Earth's surface. Dust particles are raised to higher troposphere levels by turbulent mixing and convective updrafts. They are then carried by wind for spans of time and distance, depending on their mass and meteorological conditions, before being pulled by gravity back down to Earth's surface.

The Great Source sends winds of change to shake us out of our inertia and guide us toward the life we were meant to live, a journey of reveling in the brilliance of what lies untapped within us. When our lifetimes end and the dust settles, what remains are our lessons and the love we carry onward. During our time, ours is to transcend shame and immerse ourselves in mystery, love ourselves, and bring forth extraordinary wisdom. We become complete by freely forgiving, sowing self-compassion, and claiming our birthright of self-love without limits, which we will do until we are done.

Between Breaths

With each breath, there are two moments of stillness—between the breath you draw in and the breath you let go. In this moment, allow yourself again to follow your breathing. Notice the steady rhythm of the rising and falling of your chest. Then find the spaces between your breaths—between the breaths you take in and the ones you release. Follow a breath in and pause to capture its stillness. As you release, capture another moment of quiet. Do this a few more times until you're comfortable with it.

Now, drop further into your body. Go low, down, deeply inward. Consider the possibility that within you, there is wisdom more remarkable than the sum of all you have learned or will learn in your lifetime, that you have a brilliant intelligence beyond your own mind. Remember that with each breath, there are two moments of stillness—between the breath you draw in and the breath you release. Allow yourself again to follow your breathing in this way. Notice the steady rhythm of the rising and falling of your chest. Again, find the spaces between your breaths—between the breaths you take in and the ones you release. Follow a breath in and pause to experience stillness by pausing with it before you release it. As you release find stillness.

Pause now to attune to the subtle vibrations of your longing. Observing the flow of your breath, notice the level of effort your body is making for each inhalation and exhalation. Is the space between each breath always the same? If you were to imagine your inward breath as an uphill grade, what slope does it have? Is it steep, or perhaps gradual? Is there a peak before the air that comes in ends and the exhale of air begins? And if the outward breath was the downhill slope, what is its length and angle? When the breath reaches the bottom, how much space is there for you to land and rest? Notice your breath going in, your breath going out. Upward and pause, downward and pause. Inward, outward by the innate intelligence of your body. Just observe yourself noticing being here in this present moment.

The yearning deep within your heart is the way to knowing what you most desire—what you are here in this lifetime, by your truth, living to complete. The love that you experience inside your heart is creating vibrations that match that of your true purpose. Cultivate silence for it and bring awareness to it; savor the connection.

Let your bodily senses awaken to the clarity that they offer to you. Unfettered, they will align with this same vibration. You and your purpose are one. As you listen to each breath, ask yourself something: What is my longing wanting me to know? How can I be present to it? What do I need to listen to but have yet to hear? How do I need to be? How do I need to become? Vow to remain aware and open to receiving, and answers will come to you.

On a hot summer day, hiking at a dry mesa of the Rocky Mountain Front Range, I noticed a leaf propelled along the ground on its edge by a gentle gust of air.

Wind Invisible
Invisible, windblown soul,
birthed by Love's intention,
fluidly in motion, perpetually impermanent,
longing, drifting, strengthening,
harnessing invisible wind.
You do and you be,
you cease to return to be,
by wind invisible
rendered the true you sought,
sans suffering, complete.

Last Breaths

The gift of knowing the preciousness of life often comes to us by the final actions of our elders. For several months, my mother, then 89, had been in a hospice facility near her home in Chesterfield, Missouri. Over our lives together, Mom and I offered and accepted each other's forgiveness; we had made our amends for past hurts we had caused one another. I was grateful that we had.

One weekend afternoon in May 2020, news came from my sister, who had been very attentive to the care of her, that Mom had become comatose and would not live more than a few days, and that I should come as quickly as possible. I told her that I didn't feel a need to. That I had made peace and there was nothing left to do or say. I was hedging on the inevitable. Besides, I added, it was a long drive, more than 800 miles from Colorado. Amid the onset of the COVID-19 outbreak, flight travel had become scarcer and more complicated. I explained that I'd wait and make the drive later, at Mom's funeral. My sister had zero tolerance for my quibbling. She laid out my options: "Get in your car and drive here to see your mother one last time. This is something you have to do for yourself, for Mom, and for your children." She was right. This was legacy. Within minutes, I had tossed some things in a bag and was driving on I-70 east bound.

A day later I arrived at my mother's hospice room where I found my sister and some of my other family members. She appeared to be unconscious; she was lying still in her bed. Her breathing shallow. My sister and one brother left to have dinner, leaving another brother and me with our mother.

Alone at her deathbed, my brother and I sat by our mother's side. It was quiet, only occasional murmurs outside the room. No machines or medications, just the three of us waiting, on the cusp of witnessing a mystery—the moment of her death.

Phyllis Irene Wallace had strawberry blonde hair and a freckled Scots Irish complexion. She was beautiful, poised, articulate, and vivacious. Her curiosity, kindness, and adventurous nature shone through her radiant blue eyes. She was a stylish dresser and a stickler for good hair. My paternal grandpa had aptly nicknamed her "Peaches." Although, in her advanced age, she had let concerns about her beauty fade. Apparently, she was coming to terms with attending to her soul and readying herself for a new dimension she was soon to enter. She kept her attention on the essentials.

As an hour passed, our concentration was squarely on Mom. My brother and I sat side-by-side in stillness. Inside though, I was filled with sadness, anticipation, gratitude, and awe. The more I sat with her and watched her, the more I saw Mom as brave preparing to leave an existence that she had fulfilled and had helped many others fulfil for themselves; she was beginning her adventure into another realm.

Each breath became noticeably shallower and more labored, now occupying a distinguishable arc slowly leading from one into the next, with the spaces between each one growing longer. My brother and I began counting the time between them, closely listening for muted sounds of air coming into and going out of her, watching intently as her chest rose and fell. My brother and I were counting in whispers to one another and telling our Mom how we loved her and appreciated her and all that she had done for us throughout our lives.

We counted three, five, and eventually ten seconds between her breaths. Across a lifetime of actively mothering six children, devoting herself as grandmother of thirteen, and working tirelessly for her livelihood and for charitable causes, back then ten seconds passed like a blink. Now, ten seconds seemed to take forever. There was nothing to do except surrender and watch her go. I eventually found myself encouraging her to go. Great spans of fifteen seconds were now elapsing between her breaths. Three of them came and went. And then, none. No air was coming or going. No rising or falling of her chest. Mom's body was, at last, entirely still. She left with grace.

But around that moment something else we couldn't see was also taking place.

Her body was taken away. I needed some fresh air and some time alone. Descending a nearby staircase, I felt an onrush—a swirling cloud of amber, peach, pink, and white—enveloped by love, warmth, and kindness. I'm sure that was my mom's essence, radiating right there, on Earth, one last time. Thrilled and honored, I was filled with joy. About a week later, she would come to me in a dream as a swoosh of orange, in and out like a swiftly flying swallow. I felt as if she was thanking me and bidding "so long for now." On that day in May it was her time, and she allowed me to witness her gracefully surrender— one final gesture of generosity for which I am forever grateful.

The poignancy of death surfaces wisdom on life and living. That moment of being at my mom's hospice bedside lives within me in ways that I know clearly now and in other ways I might never know. Part of what I know is that as I enter the autumn of my life, I possess a vitality that is mine to align with, know well, and live out, by following where my soul's longing might lead.

***

The human heart thumps to its own biological beats, an intricate and interconnected four measure rhythm pumping life-giving oxygen to the body and getting rid of carbon dioxide waste without needing the mind to do anything. The right half of the heart, the atrium, receives deoxygenated blood returning from the body's cells, pushing it into the lungs so carbon dioxide can be exhaled. The left side, the ventricle, draws in newly oxygenated red blood cells from the lungs and propels them out across the body, keeping the blood nourished. This symphony is a testament to the body's elegant simplicity—a graceful intelligence where all we must do to make it work is breathe.

Similarly refined and reflexive is the nature of the Self eternally seeking bliss. Thoughts and feelings are pulses that may enliven, or they may diminish us. Like the air we breathe emotions flow into the body and are held while mindful consciousness seins them for meaning. All a person must do to learn and grow from our endless flow of feelings is to become aware of them, feel them, and understand them. The self can flourish into its higher level of being by the collective memories cultivated from its rich flow of emotions.

What are you circulating? What do you hold onto? Refuse to let go of? What can you release? What will you draw into yourself? What is the current state of your thinking mind? Of your emotional mind? And, of your body mind? How do you nourish each one? How might you ignore or neglect them? By courage, intentionally letting go, and following the summons of the spiritual rhythm pulsing within is the most powerful act of living.

I invite you, in this moment, to pause and reflect. As soon as you finish reading this sentence listen within yourself . . . What do you notice? What is going on inside you? How does it feel? If it was a weather pattern, how would the sky look? What would be the temperature? Are you uncomfortable or are you enjoying this moment? What's the forecast? How do you feel about what's ahead? Regardless of the weather, be it turbulent or calm, as you attune to it and navigate to be where you need to be at the right time is being present and mindful of what is within you.

All power to succeed in our life's purpose lies within us. With unwavering conviction, we can trust that each step taken toward our true calling responds to a longing from the depths of our soul. To truly understand this truth, think back to a time in your life when you were completely and genuinely happy. What emotions were you experiencing? Where in your body did you feel the intensity of that joy? How did it feel to be in that state of mind? How did your body react? Who were you being at that moment? What would your loved ones say about the person you were then? What would you want that version of yourself to know? When your thoughts, feelings, and physical sensations align, give yourself permission to cherish them. This way of being is just one more avenue for finding contentment. Take a moment to appreciate yourself for recognizing and learning from that moment of joy that you had created.

Chapter Twelve

In Forgiving

Love is that condition in the healing spirit so profound that it allows us to forgive.

— Maya Angelou

English poet, translator, and satirist of the Enlightenment era, Alexander Pope, famously observed, "To err is human; to forgive, divine." What would happen if you extended this grace to yourself freely all the time, any time? How would it feel to forgive yourself for all your mistakes? What changes might you notice in how you interact with others, and in general, throughout your life? Why not give it a go right now?

Self-forgiveness is a path of personal healing, growth, and wisdom that begins with understanding and accepting the past as it is. It's not about covering up what has happened, rationalizing, or avoiding: it's about understanding and coming to terms with one's own actions, thoughts, feelings, and regrets. This calls for a willingness to explore the original intentions behind the actions and the patience to reconcile the difference between what was intended and what happened. From there we'll find greater self-acceptance and can commit to expressing ourselves in a more authentic and loving way and with clarity and integrity in the future. In forgiving ourselves we set ourselves free. And the process is simple.

Recall a recent conflict that you experienced with someone you care about—your child, a friend, or your partner—who sincerely forgave you for your part. And you sincerely forgave them for their part. But, before you forgave one another, you worked through the conflict together, each owning your piece, listening, and expressing your emotions. After you forgave one another, how did you feel about them? About yourself? Here are some possibilities: closer, free, relaxed, trusting, responsible, capable, accepting, and safe. What else might you have felt by forgiving and receiving forgiveness?

Remember another recent time when you were struggling, and you spoke unkindly to yourself. We can be so hard on ourselves when we make mistakes or feel not good enough. Recall the emotions it brought up. How did you feel in that moment as both the sender and receiver? Can you feel a pull from the past? Maybe a time when you felt that same way as a child?

Place your hands together over your heart space, in the center of your chest. Then take a deep breath, focus on your heart area and reach out to the innocent child inside you who heard those words, or ones similar to them, recently and long ago. Take a moment to look into their eyes. If it were possible to travel back in time, what would you want that child to know? What do you want them to understand? How would you like to show them love? Speak quietly to them, aloud or in your mind, as you stay focused on your heart.

Now turn to your adult self and the recent instance of speaking harshly to yourself. What would you do differently if you could go back to that time? Freeze the moment, and now offer yourself compassion and understanding. Express your regrets. Take responsibility for your words. Acknowledge what was going on for you leading up to and in that moment—how overwhelmed, frustrated, or impatient you were feeling with yourself. Sit with any remorse and any empathy you have for yourself right now and let it sink in. What else might you need to repair the part of you that was hurt? Ask for forgiveness and give it time to settle in for healing to unfold.

Forgiveness is an act of healing—it sets us free. Whenever we grant ourselves forgiveness, we engage in a powerful and courageous act of self-love imbued with the power to change our perceptions entirely. Jacques Lusseyran, a blind French Resistance leader during World War II, captured this beautifully when reflecting on his Nazi interrogation. He described discovering a transformative, "miraculous healing remedy" freely available within each of us—a gift from the Great Light that resides in us all. This healing force, he explained, "lives in the fact that you breathe and have blood pulsing in your temples." And, if you pay strict attention to your moments of suffering as such, divine forgiveness can exponentially enfold you in love's nurturance: "There is forgiveness for every misery. And as misery grows, forgiveness grows along with it."

Forgiving yourself is indeed an extraordinary act of love that is, by its very nature, expansive: It can happen simply by suggestion. Simply suggesting forgiving oneself instantly begins momentum to swing open the door to self-acceptance and step into enduring spiritual attunement. One's first step begins by listening to inner rhythm of love vying for expression through forgiveness—a radical act of spiritual liberation— drumming peace forth by the beat of one's own natural rhythm of the boundless love harbored within. In this way, forgiveness is both an intention and an action for personal liberation.

We are shaped by accumulated layers upon layers of experience and infused with knowledge by our unique lessons we are each here to learn from. Stored within the recesses of our minds are the past record of each persona we've lived out in prior lifetimes holding the memories created by each of them. These influence the person we are today. From the early days of infancy to the aureate years of old age, each phase is waiting to become activated and present opportunities for advancing our evolution. As we tend to our emotional injuries by forgiving ourselves, we actively build a stronger and more resilient whole. Every part within you welcomes this kind of forgiveness sentiment directly from you to you, expressed by words like these:

I am sorry for your suffering.

Please forgive me for ever ignoring, judging, or rejecting you.
I deeply admire you for your courage and resilience, and for bringing us to healing.
I respect you,
I love you,
I thank you.

There are no rules, no obligation to forgive yourself or anyone else. You owe this to no one. Forgiving is entirely optional. If you don't know how or aren't ready yet, be patient and wait until, and if, you are. In the meantime, you can set a loving intention to *be ready* to forgive.

As you care for yourself through forgiveness, the eternal flame within you grows brighter. It is sourced within you and can never be extinguished. So, make a pledge to love yourself. Pledge to show yourself compassion. Pledge to forgive yourself again and again to regain and reignite your vital force.

Self-forgiveness opens a path home to our true selves. By forgiving, we strengthen our stillness—we give up the need for stories of hurts and disappointments. If we want to forgive, we must show ourselves kindness and understanding.

***

The following is another way of bringing forth forgiveness. *Ho'oponopono* is a traditional Hawaiian practice of reconciliation, forgiveness, and healing, with deep spiritual and cultural roots. Hawaiian peoples have used it to resolve intra- and interpersonal conflicts, restore harmony within families, and promote emotional healing. Ho'oponopono is translated, according to author Ulrich Dupree, as "returning to the Divine plan or, the path to perfection."

To best prepare for this self-guided personal Ho'oponopono commit to allowing yourself to simply be in acceptance. Be willing to suspend any judgment by gently reminding yourself to be open to whatever comes.

Begin by following the sibilation of your breathing: its ebb and flow like a calm seaside breeze. Turn your attention inward. What do you notice? Observe the rhythm of your breathing and the beating of your heart. Place a hand on your heart space at the center of your chest. Gaze softly down for a moment to notice your hand rising and falling as your hand rises and falls with each breath, for three more breaths. Notice what happens beneath your palm. What words would describe it? Pause for a moment. What else can you feel in your heart space there, just beneath your hand? Feel the longing emanating from beneath your hand, melancholy and wistful, as if you are homesick for a connection to a place you once knew well, a place you once held as dear and as sacred. Forgiveness can bring you closer to that.

Allow affection for yourself to gradually seep into your heart as seawater seeps into the sand. Recall a recent incident where you were unkind to yourself. Can you remember where you were? What did you do then? How did that make you feel in the moment? Did you say anything to yourself in that moment? And how did you feel about yourself afterward? Now, as you recall that time, can you notice what emotions are arising for you—restlessness, impatience, intrigue, boredom, frustration, serenity? Simply observe whatever it is without reacting. Take a few moments to consider that you might release any need to hang on to those old memories and feelings. With your hand on your heart as you focus on your breath, move through the four steps of this forgiveness experience. Pause after each of the four phrases to allow your words to sink into your heart.

I am sorry for . . .

Refer to the memory you just recalled. Acknowledge any pain or hurt you felt or harsh words you said to yourself. Then, complete this next step.

I accept and forgive you for . . .

Allow yourself a moment of compassion, to atone for whenever and however you have held yourself as less than anything other than lovable. On your exhales, release the blame that you have for yourself. On your inhales, draw in compassion for yourself. As you notice yourself softening, repeat the following to yourself.

Thank you, I appreciate you for . . .

Be specific, trusting that whatever comes into your mind with kindness is the right thing. Consider telling yourself this: "Thank you. I appreciate your courage, vulnerability, curiosity, compassion, empathy, humor, warmth, and openness."

To complete: *I love you, just as you are.*

Let the words sink in fully. Say it as many times as it takes to feel its truth. It might take more time than you expect, but accept that and keep saying it until it seeps in. Push through any barriers that might prevent you from accepting your own kindness. Take a full breath. Feel your own unconditional love for yourself.

Feel the spreading warmth of your own love. As you speak words of kindness to yourself, let them enter your open heart. The gift you give yourself nourishes and invigorates. Remember that whenever you are hurting, you can always forgive yourself by reciting the four Ho'oponopono forgiveness phrases:

I am sorry.
Please forgive me.
Thank you.
I love you.

We are all walking, breathing vessels of wisdom and love, awaiting, and earning our release to infinite bliss. When I remember this, it rouses my vitality for living. It inspires me to unleash my essence and call on its boundless strength to live it out in whatever way I might create. I know that this cycle of going into dimness and figuring how to reconnect to Light, is why I came here.

There are times, usually when I'm under-resourced, at my lesser moments, that I either don't believe that, or I forget that it's true. So, I lapse and slip, and life gets heavy and harder than it needs to be. When I am present to myself, I've learned by years of practice, to go to ways that I know will bring me into stillness, to heal, and "lighten up." Even when slipping, every cell of my body remembers the way out and it relentlessly calls to me listen; my soul calls me to remember the different way. I have come to trust this—that my soul will never stop longing for me to listen and follow and know peace. In the rest of the time that I have, I've vowed to keep listening, opening, and finding stillness in myself and to remember that there is that Great stillness within all others of us.

The choice to reclaim our state of self-lovingness is ours to make at any time. It is our sacred obligation to shed the old and to claim new ways to self-liberation. We start by listening for our inner whisperings calling us to connect to the personal guidance that awaits.

Consider actively calling for guidance. You might have your own way, or you might use words like these:

Accompany me, Spirit. Guide me through the changes awaiting me. Spirit, guide me through the inevitable fields of uncertainty in life. I know that I will face adversity. I know, too, that there will be times for celebration, joy, and gratitude. Guide me to be present to all of it and to accept, learn, and integrate the wisdom that all my experiences offer me. Imbue me with love and light. Anchor me in the assurance of my own self-love. I know that the love I cultivate within my being matches the frequency of divine love—it is of the same, Source. Remind me to trust this inherently and to know it instinctively.

As I go forward in life, I promise to keep awakening to vitality of love. I trust that my soul longs to bring me to love. I vow to cherish love as intrinsic to the vitality of my whole being. I vow to embrace my unique way of knowing what love is and how it comes by my inner truth. Let my passion be as seamless as calm breezes, inwardly flowing within myself and outwardly flowing from myself to others I love. Ultimately, I know that there is nothing for me to fear, and though I might, from time to time, forget that I ask that you remind me when I do. I promise to keep myself alert to your touches by the natural longing of my being a soul embodied seeking perfection in love.

A New Love

The path of the soul-bound hero begins by her attuning to the calling of her heart. She may at times, become confused and forget how real this is, even find herself lost in this world. Forgetting momentarily her truth, she risks falling prey to illusions. Unknowingly, she invents alternative realities by acting out roles inauthentic to her essence. Retreading old ones from her past might seem okay; it is after all, familiar. So, for a time, she goes on, blinded and not knowing better. Then she remembers who she truly is, re-awakens to her essence, and empathically reclaims her commitment to do and become her highest version of herself. She forgives herself. She realizes that she had only forgotten. Once again poised, she returns to the way of her true Self, and continues finding her way by closely listening to her quiet voice within.

Darker corners within you though often painful, possess treasures—starlight waiting to shine. The ultimate human goal is becoming radiant with the unlimited source of spiritual light imbued within each of us. The often-untapped superpower stands ready to light you up. How clear is your own sense of this? Do you remember it?

***

The act of healing is mysterious—an alchemy of lived pain, brain memory, and love. Pause now to feel into your own ready flow of healing light within yourself. There it is, a felt sensation within you. Set an open hand upon it. Breathe into and out of that space. Call to it, your mystery. Call it forth and meet it with declarations of love: "I love you. I need you. I welcome you. Come here!" Move into the space with tenderness and care. Although you might feel at times forgotten and alone, you are not. Reach out to any of the pained parts of you; they may be as if small children crying out for healing. Rescue your children within, orphaned in despair and loneliness. No longer to be questioning, hoping, striving.

Gather your love and understanding. There is likely at least one inner child within you needing more love. Talk to them. You might say something like, "Come to me child. I promise to respect, embrace, and love you as I can." Tenderly, again, whisper words in your own name to yourself, such as, "I know you deserve love. I do love you. I love you for now and forever. Though at times, I forget, now, and many times from now, I vow to forgive, rejoin, and continue loving you."

By acknowledging and expressing love toward yourself, you tap into the unshakable truth that your being is composed of love. Just as your body is nourished by the flow of your blood, your entire being is fed by the flow of your affection. Your love originates directly from the spark of Great within you, and it is endless.

As you allow the flow, even if only briefly, notice subtle vibrations that come to you. You may sense that you are aligning yourself with a new kind of love. Taking time to be present with yourself this way is an act of alignment. Breathe deeply and intentionally, allowing yourself to fully embody this loving way.

Precious Being
The boy kicks a tin can, it holds nothing,
though his heart is full.
Time fades to see without eyes.

Longing

Adversity adds the edge upon which he is to balance
mining precious moments between trials.
To ascend he must know what isn't.
Then brave someday surrender,
to welcome adversity's way,
to endure danger,
to fade no more to fate's past,
to know his true, good, beautiful within,
to wonder and to follow the Secret Teacher of him.
Though by time, by doubt will linger,
vexed by villains forgetting, neglecting, and forsaking.
Follows on though by flight and flow
vibration,
resonance,
music,
to listen
to know
witness by breathing,
   in stillness,
over and over, and reveal
his precious being.

Chapter Thirteen

Soul Genius

Comets in our Milky Way are masses of ice, dust, and rocky particulates, like a gigantic dirty snowball in the vacuum of space that, when warmed by passing too close to the sun's heat will vaporize. As their once-volatile ice boils away, the comet will eventually disintegrate, leaving only a rocky core to be absorbed into the vastness of space. Before it dies, it flies toward the warming sun and releases a dense cloud of water, carbon dioxide, and other gases. These spew off from its evaporating nucleus, forming a tail of bright dust, an endless comma, that stretches behind it for as long as 40,000 kilometers—this tailing dust is the brilliant light of a comet that we can see with our eyes alone.

Just as a dying comet yields its light to the flight of time and space, the soul releases its accumulated power to something far greater. We are all light beings moving toward sacred completion. Particles and gases from the harmful etchings of our unconscious to our exalted moments of loving perfection—all we have experienced: our joys and sorrows, wounds and wonders—become luminous fragments, our evaporating dust tailings, woven into the fabric of universal wisdom

In choosing to incarnate, our souls have exercised free will. They intend to complete the ultimate flight. At the farthest reach of our journey, the heroic soul longs to merge with the Self, to rise in perfect unity with the cosmic Great Love—the source we are ever seeking to truly know.

Nested within each of us is a spark of the Great Love, patiently awaiting our full trust and unbridled connection. A divine pinwheel of pure vitality, it is our shimmering essence. We hold this effervescent, vibrating spark of Light within our physical bodies—it is our prana, our life force. It radiates outward too, forming each of our unique auras. Every higher purpose-driven breath we take, every choice we make to live and to love, nourishes it. The more attuned we become to it, the more vivid our experience of its presence—and the more fully we live from it.

Sometimes, you may feel it as a great rush—a surge of energy, a gentle breeze, or a powerful current. The Light within is always moving, always creating life and love. It is awakening you to your true nature, calling you again and again to merge with it. It speaks to your deepest purpose in this lifetime. It is what you've been longing for—now, and in every life before.

At times, the Light within whispers—fervent as a newborn's cry, or soft as a breeze. It never calls in desperation, but to bring you closer to vitality, joy, love, and freedom. It will never abandon you. It will not give itself over to the illusion of separation. It waits within, inviting you to venture into your depths.

Creativity finds form in the unity of conflicting forces. Genius evolves by the wisdom created through wedding our passions and devotions with our willingness to surrender to forces beyond our imaginations assuming form within. We grow through harmonizing melodies of tension competing— between boldness and hesitancy, shock and serenity, being grounded and untethered, hopelessness and optimism, trust and suspicion, pessimism and sanguinity. Such is the nature of the universal polarized creative forces of earth, air, fire, and water, of feminine and of masculine, of yin and of yang, of life and of death. As human embodiments of light polarities, we exist to experience the tension of living in a body accommodating all universal forces where ultimately harmony will prevail and become our natural state as we come to rest within the mystery of conflicting forces. Then rest in this mystery.

Leaving Love
Taking what you can, avoiding the rest,
such is the accidental life.
Patient purpose awaits its time,
steeped for you to know truth,
in unison with the Great.
So now, take one step with grace,
another with determination.
You'll not go wrong knowing
the difference between a life and living is,
the love you leave behind.
The difference between you and Divine
are the smudges you keep
on the window to
your soul.

The longing of the soul's desire for love can make life uncomfortable. We live at the crossroads of ruins: of our past that must go out of us for enlightenment to come into us. It's a big stretch we must complete, as Emerson observed: "Every soul is by this intrinsic necessity quitting its whole system of things, its friends and home and law and faith, as the shellfish crawls out of its beautiful but stony case, because it no longer admits of its growth, and slowly forms a new house." Upon transformation, the person we have become today barely recognizes our person of yesterday. At times we're unsure how to even be the new us.

Each of us embarks on our own unique heroic quest to know our own unique truth—this noblest quest—to fulfill the great purpose of our existence. Along the way we can get wracked by its mystery, complexion, and confusion. Doubt of all kinds can crop up in our minds, complicate, and mess with our outlook. As, in the words of writer Anne Lamott: "Life is such a mystery that you have to wonder if God drinks a little." But, if it were the other way around and we always knew the next step to take, we'd miss endless opportunities to stretch our capacity for free-will choosing and we'd miss the building of strength that comes by believing in oneself, by taking a stand for our expansion, by being brave when fear shows up (as it always does). We'd also miss out on endless opportunities to absorb ourselves in learning how to be ourselves, and in chasing what inspires us, and in engaging our hearts, mind, body, and Spirit in all that intrigues us. With each courageous step into uncharted territory, dormancy yields to vitality, and qualities already within us awaken and embolden—courage, wisdom, self-confidence, curiosity, vulnerability, exploration, and so many more—all to serve and compensate when we are willing to risk becoming who we are. Each time we add to our reservoir of wisdom we serve the evolution of our soul.

***

It takes immense pressure, over one to three billion years, for pure carbon within Earth to become a diamond, the most enduring material in nature. The markings and inclusions on each stone signify its age, shape, and ability to sparkle and capture and break waves of light brilliantly. The journey to reach your brilliance within you must be done over and over, repeatedly, under the pressure of living, until you create your own well-worn path to it where then rediscovering it becomes easier.

    I invite you in this moment to turn toward the sensation of your longing. Start by feeling your way to it. Intuitively, you know how. Listen for its gentle, ceaseless whisper, asking you to return and to reconnect with it. Feel the yearning you have for this, your own source of truth. Your longing is eternal, and so are you. Breathe into it. Be with it in stillness. Feed its ever-growing appetite through the inherent grace of your presence right now.

Acting as if it is a living, breathing entity, ask whatever you want to know of it. Then, listen and receive its response.

Your longing is of your soul calling you to be present. It wants you to live your life with purpose. Though it might have been layered over, you do know your purpose. Pause a moment and take a few deep breaths. Close your eyes and ask to be shown your purpose, then listen closely. Attend to what will come to you naturally and effortlessly as you breathe and turn inward to the quiet space behind your closed eyelids. The answer to your question will ring with notes of compassion and a felt sense of knowing. Never forceful, never impatient or imposing, yet always calm, patient, and available to support you. This is Source acting within you, aware of every pain you have endured and every struggle you have encountered across all lifetimes. It is ready to guide you throughout this lifetime.

Nourishment comes from the intensity and depth of commitment to following the path of longing. The culmination of all experiences, including those of loneliness, abandonment, betrayal, and aimlessness, serve to strengthen and expand our capacity to embrace more of the variety offered in this lifetime. It is here, now, in this moment, making its offering for you to know the ancient Great within.

Love of the Great has always been within you. It was there at times that you felt like giving up. It was there when you felt confused, awkward, and doubtful. It was there when, alone, you intensely wished for love. It was with you at times when you behaved recklessly and hurt others or yourself. At moments of great shame, it was there with acceptance and sympathy. You have never been alone; even in your darkest nights, your soul, that spark of love inside you is there. Listen to its subtle call.

Your soul is calling for you to accept its invitation of partnership and active participation in your life journey. I encourage you to again pause and listen closely for this gentle whisper that has always been within you. It may be a tangible sensation felt within your heart, at the top of your head, or along your spine. Place one of your hands on the area where you sense the most aliveness and notice the sensations. Speak to it gently; welcome its presence, and if resistance arises, include that too. It's all part of the experience.

Within you is your soul, eager to join you in active partnership. Imagine it there in whatever form comes to you. Grasp the outstretched hand of your soul and stand side by side, united for this lifetime and beyond. Feel the strength within you, ready to take your next steps in life, intimately joined together. Your soul awaits your vow, or perhaps for you to renew your vow, to venture forth in ways to continue revitalizing and enriching you.

Being this way with yourself is to be self-loving. As awareness of this presence-seeking wholeness expands, the flatness from simply coping with life goes away. Opening to becoming self-loving opens new realms of regeneration, where the pain and regret of the past drift away and the wisdom of their lessons live on. You can always reach into this ever-unfolding mystery of life with firm commitment, owning your direction in life to be on point, on purpose, and on mission. Brace yourself for a bold transformation.

Chapter Fourteen
Waves of Light

Each of us is a dynamic shifting interplay of light and shadow. Imagine, that within yourself is an ever-changing, multicolored spiral—rotating and flowing simultaneously with emotions and all you have lived through, of your inimitable past and present. Within your spiral lie points that are quietly calling for expression, calling for healing. Soul, the wellspring of wisdom, softly beckons you to listen and receive its guidance. Yet, in our modern world, endless distractions—many just a fingertip away—tempt us to numb or ignore this sacred calling.

The truth is beautifully simple: there is no grand effort required for healing to unfold. All that is needed is the invitation of silence and the cultivation of emptiness. By listening to the subtle voice within and aligning our lives with its rhythm, the true self emerges—flowing naturally and effortlessly.

To begin this journey, I invite you to find a quiet place, a moment just for you. Be tender with yourself, and as you read these words of the soul aloud, let them resonate deeply within you.

**

Listen closely, listen attentively. Listen to know my language. I may not convey to you direct by words. I may come into you by the way of your dreams, I may come by spoken metaphor, I may come by symbols you see, I may come to you by moments of synchronicity. I am of Source, subtle and unique. I provide you inner knowing. I am the mystical being of wisdom within you. I defy human limitations of body, time, and space. By me you are never alone.

You have been taught to believe that you are captive to a brain and that the source of your life springs from your body alone. I want you to know that I am so much more, that you are so much more. I am your life source, and we are irretrievably connected. Your body feels my influence. I affect all layers of your being—I secure your physical, I feed your vital prana, stimulate your sensation and mind, infuse your wisdom, and encourage your bliss. However, I am not of any one of them. I embrace and exist within them all and outside of them—I am clear and pure vibration.

We are of one and the same essence. We need each other to survive and to fully thrive in this lifetime that you have chosen together with me as your innermost guide. I am devoted to your wellbeing. It is through me that you long for what you are here now to experience and know for our eternal advancement. Through me, you come to your longing and learn how to honor and serve it. I am the source of your deepest knowledge. I strive to immerse you in your life purpose and ignite you to it. I will do so, by means joy and, if needed, by duress. I am the welcoming bed of your love to be gifted, first and foremost, to yourself and then to be shared with others as you may decide. You grow and thrive through me. I want only that for you. I want only that for us. As all love begins from within, I am your direct connection to its source.

Your quest in your lifetime is finding the ways into loving yourself as you are, and will become. It is yours to learn and to follow my voice, your secret teacher within, until my voice becomes your own. Though your logic-driven mind may, by fear, occasionally attempt to move you away from your essence and your love may wane, its duality and your innate search for love is part of our original agreement. You are here to rediscover the joy of loving yourself and to fully live from its source in this lifetime, and forever. Your logical mind offers great value in support of our mission—acting as your benevolent assistant—to direct and protect your energy for the work you must do. It is to ensure that you rest and make time for enjoyment, and most important, to find creative ways for you to know yourself: by this you will find your entry to your natural state of bliss. We are a seamless unit—a team united by and existing in love!

Love is your supreme gift to enjoy; it is the absolute source of your vitality. At times, you forget how to accept and to love yourself. By forgetting you banish yourself from the pleasure of paradise within your being. From your births you began learning to forget so that you could learn to remember your way back to Divine Love again and again. Doing this your true, ultimate orientation becomes etched into your eternal memory. Just as Earth orbits the Sun, you become held secure upon an axis of love. In remembering your suffering and forgiving and healing yourself you transform the lowest vibration, shame, into the highest vibration, love. Our shared ascension comes through your mastering this cycle of forgetting your essence (descent into shame) and remembering your essence (ascent into love). Your lifetime, here and now, provides this paradox so that your wisdom can expand in depth and breadth. In coming home to your true self, you complete your purpose of becoming love incarnate and absolute.

***

Our innate healing forces become engaged in moments of stillness. At this moment, I invite you to savor some stillness. Begin by shifting your focus inward and becoming aware of any place within you that is needing love. Pause as you draw in and release a full deep breath. Notice any sensations you're having, any emotions, any thoughts, any vibrations. Notice where these are coming from. Literally or figuratively, place a reassuring hand there and send a full breath to it.

Remaining aware of that memory, tune into another part of yourself that you experience as calm. Moving slowly, feel your way toward that calmness, knowing that it can bring you healing and that it already intuitively knows how to comfort you. As you move closer to it, listen for the subtle voice of your loving heart calling to you. You must feel for it. Closely listen with your body, knowing that your loving heart speaks through your sensations. Feel deeply: where within you do you ache? Breathe tenderly into that space. To heal is to love, and to love is to heal. Trust your intuition to guide you to healing.

Within you lies a quiet stillness, beyond the reach of words, waiting to be reborn in this moment. As you sit in stillness, breathe deeply, and patiently await any guiding or comforting thought, feeling of warmth that may gently arise within yourself—you are simply knowing, simply being. In the serenity of silence, your longing softly invites you to reconnect with it; your divine spark waits for you to again witness your brilliance. Notice its subtle vibration within your body. Allow your intuition to lead you to it. Allow yourself to feel your way into the calm, quiet rhythm of your longing. This is you loving yourself—gently yet powerfully—opening to your own essence, your own vibrations of healing. Feel: where within do you ache? Breathe deep into that space. Continue to feel your way into the calmness of your own longing. Feel its subtle vibration in your body. This is you loving yourself—gently yet powerfully—you are opening yourself to your own vibrations of healing. To heal is to love, to love is to heal.

As you continue opening to yourself, what sensations are you aware of? Keep feeling your way inward. Breathe fully in and out, patiently waiting and being still within yourself. In the depths of you, there is calmness that words cannot quite describe. This is the vibration of the Great in the language of your longing, your divine spark patiently waiting in stillness for you to join it, to be present to it. Breathe deep into it, draw in a full breath and completely release your breath, and then draw another full breath in, hold it a moment, and then let it go all the way out of you. Do this as many times as feels right for you in this moment.

Remember: when lost, become still. It is through calmness that we find our way back to our true home. As turbulence and distraction of life come, you can return—gently and powerfully—to the stilled calm of loving yourself. When feeling alone or overwhelmed, fatigued, or numb, whenever your heart aches, you can return to your own place of healing within. Be still, call, and wait for healing to come by your divine light, as it always will.

It is our truest nature to be kind, understanding, and loving toward ourselves, and to others. Sometimes we fear our own power, and its intensity; we fear becoming overwhelmed by our own power. Many of us were not guided or could learn from our caregivers how to summon this healing power. Imagine if we had? As we reintroduce ourselves to it, naturally it might feel a bit strange. But whenever we need to, we can grant ourselves permission to love ourselves completely, without shame.

Each time that you consciously attend to your breathing, you open yourself to your source of immense untapped energy bubbling up from within you. You enhance your partnership with your ever-patient divine spark waiting for you to claim your brilliance. It has the capacity to bring you more joy than you might ever have imagined possible. In this moment pause to feel the sensation of stillness arising from inner confidence that comes with the acceptance of your own gentle nature. From past conditioning you might feel some apprehension about this capacity that you have, but now the power of its energy is too great to resist. As you wish, you can allow walls of fear and hesitation to melt away. As you explore the depths of your wellspring of self-love, in this moment and at any other time, you can choose and allow yourself to be filled with an abundance of self-love, self-compassion, and self-acceptance for they are of the powerful being that you are. The soul has an insatiable appetite for renewal. You are imbued with its power ready to engage yourself in lifelong discovery of its mystery and intrigue. Your soul invites you to join with it in the relentless pursuit of luscious love.

Remind yourself that our collective destiny, of which you are a vital part, is to embrace ourselves and all our experiences without holding back our power to do so. We must refuse to waste these precious moments and strive to become what our soul is wanting us to know and to become. Courageously, we can rise, take hold, leave behind shame, darkness, and doubt and stand eye-level with our brilliance, and lay claim to our true essence within.

You and I have a lot ahead of us.

JFK and Oswald Are Friends
Where JFK and Oswald are friends,
and militias rust in peace.
Where words are revered of: Gandhi, Isis, Jesus, Mary Magdalene, Artemis, Mohammed, Buddha,
Rumi, Black Elk, King Jr., Chavez, and Emerson.
Where night becomes day and our dimness aflame,
Where tracks of our tears teach us.
Where our pasts and presents, yin and yang, merge as one.
Where we eclipse spinning, void of separateness, breathing of air ceases.
Where we sit with our lost dogs and in peace with those of us, we thought were lost from us.
Where we are as ever, as we had hoped.

April 30, 2022
Salida, Colorado

About the Author

Christopher Sansone is a life, leadership, and spiritual coach dedicated to helping others know and embrace their purpose and live with love, guided by their soul's calling. As a practitioner of spiritual regression and intentional soul states, he offers a holistic and highly effective path to deep healing, wellbeing, and growth. With a PhD in Human Development from Fielding Graduate Institute and coaching certification from the Co-Active Training Institute (CTI), Chris integrates spiritual insight, psychological depth, and practical wisdom to support individuals and groups on their transformational journeys.

His commitment to leadership, racial equity, and belonging is rooted in his own spiritual development and reflected in his peer-reviewed articles and ongoing work to foster just and inclusive communities. When he's not coaching, writing, or teaching, you'll mostly find him spending time with his family, practicing tai chi and yoga, painting, fly fishing for mountain trout, hiking the Rockies, or rowing at McIntosh Lake near his Colorado home—where he finds the balance and inspiration, and he loves to help others discover theirs.

From the Author: Thank you for purchasing *Longing: A Pilgrimage to your Quiet Power Within*. My sincere hope is that you derived as much from reading this book as I did in creating it. If you have a few moments, please feel free to add your review of the book to your favorite online site.

To discover how I can support your transformation or to sign up for my newsletter please visit www.LiveLifeSoul.com.

References

Introduction

Newberg, Andrew, and Mark Robert Waldman. *How Enlightenment Changes Your Brain: The New Science of Transformation.* New York: Avery, 2016. This book investigates the neurological basis of enlightenment experiences, combining scientific research with practical exercises to explore how such moments of heightened awareness and spirituality can alter the brain and transform life which he also discusses at a *Sense of Mind* podcast April 2022. Andrew Newberg, M.D., is widely known for his pioneering research focused on the development of neurotransmitter tracers for the evaluation of religiosity, to which he refers to as "neurotheology." Newberg has published numerous books, which have been translated into several different languages, and authored over 250 peer reviewed articles and chapters on brain function.

Pew Research Center of spirituality in the U.S., was conducted July 31-Aug. 6, 2023, among a nationally representative sample of 11,201; *Spirituality Among Americans*; pewresearch.org.

Yogananda, Paramahansa. *Autobiography of a Yogi.* 1946. Reprint, Los Angeles: Self-Realization Fellowship, 1998. This spiritual classic recounts Yogananda's journey to self-realization, offering readers insights into the ancient practices of yoga and meditation, along with intriguing stories of his encounters with spiritual teachers.

Twist, Lynne. *Living a Committed Life: Finding Freedom and Fulfillment in a Purpose Larger Than Yourself.* Oakland, CA: Berrett-Koehler Publishers, 2022. This is a semi-autobiographical account by a highly regarded author and social influencer that provides insights on how living a life devoted to a cause greater than oneself can lead to deeper meaning, purpose, and fulfillment.

Chapter One

Castaneda, Carlos. *Journey to Ixtlan: The Lessons of Don Juan.* New York: Simon & Schuster, 1972. This is the second book in Castaneda's series on his apprenticeship with the purported Yaqui shaman Don Juan Matus. It focuses on self-awareness, transformation, and breaking free from habitual ways of perceiving the world, offering a spiritual guide and a philosophical exploration of reality.

Berger, Lee R., and John Hawks. *Almost Human: The Astonishing Tale of Homo Naledi and the Discovery That Changed Our Human Story.* Washington, DC: National Geographic, 2017; recounts the groundbreaking discovery of *Homo naledi* fossils in South Africa and explores how this species has reshaped our understanding of human evolution.

Gage, Nita, and Linda Star Wolf. *Soul Whispering: The Art of Awakening Shamanic Consciousness.* Rochester, VT: Bear & Company, 2017. Two highly experienced therapists and shamanic guides explore how persons can connect with their inner wisdom and spiritual guides through shamanic practices, by awakening deeper consciousness for healing and transformation.

Hoffman, Bob. *A Path to Personal Freedom and Love.* New York: Foundation Press, 1996. The essay overviews the generational figuring of complex behaviors and beliefs and the influence of shame on personal development. It provides broad insights into the human condition and refers to a framework for understanding four aspects of being human—emotion, intellect, body, and spirit.

Huber, Cheri. *There's Nothing Wrong with You: Going Beyond Self-Hate.* Murphys, CA: Keep It Simple Books, 1997.

References

Kribbe, Pamela. *Jeshua Channelings*. Maastricht, Netherlands: Oak House Publishing, 2008. Kribbe, P. *Dark Night of the Soul*. Utrecht: J. Anker Publishers, 2008. The concept of "inherited lovelessness" is discussed in Pamela Kribbe's books, particularly these two.

Chapter Two

Burgo, Joseph. *Building Self-Esteem: How Learning from Shame Helps Us to Grow*. London: Welbeck Publishing, 2020. Burgo explores the complex relationship between shame and self-esteem, offering practical guidance on how to confront feelings of inadequacy and use them as a catalyst for personal growth and emotional resilience that he also offers at a *Sense of Mind* podcast July 2022.

Bradshaw, John. *Healing the Shame That Binds You*. Deerfield Beach, FL: Health Communications, 1988. Bradshaw was instrumental in popularizing the idea that shame can be both healthy and toxic, the latter of which binds individuals in cycles of self-hate and dysfunction. This is one among many of his writings on the adverse impact of shame.

Emerson, Ralph Waldo. *The Spiritual Emerson: Essential Writings*. Edited by David M. Robinson. Boston: Beacon Press, 2003. This edition compiles some of Emerson's most profound works exploring spirituality, self-reliance, and the divine in nature. Emerson discusses the concept of the "Oversoul" in his essay titled *The Over-Soul*, which is part of his collection *Essays: First Series* originally published in 1841.

Chapter Three

Emerson, Ralph Waldo. *The Spiritual Emerson: Essential Writings*. Edited by David M. Robinson. Boston: Beacon Press, 2003.

de Botton, Alain. *The Course of Love*. New York: Simon & Schuster, 2016. de Botton explores the realities of a long-term relationship, emphasizing that real love is less about romantic idealism and more about emotional growth, understanding, and navigating the complexities of everyday life together.

Chapter Four

Georgia M. Winters, Elizabeth L. Jeglic, Benjamin N. Johnson, Cordelia Chou, The prevalence of sexual grooming behaviors among survivors of childhood sexual abuse, Child Abuse & Neglect, Volume 154, 2024, 106842, ISSN 0145-2134 https://www.sciencedirect.com/science/article/pii/S0145213424002321

Winters, G. M., & Jeglic, E. L. (2021). The Sexual Grooming Scale – Victim Version: The Development and Pilot Testing of a Measure to Assess the Nature and Extent of Child Sexual Grooming. Victims & Offenders, 17(6), 919–940. https://doi.org/10.1080/15564886.2021.1974994

Chapter Five

Nuland, Sherwin B. *How We Die: Reflections on Life's Final Chapter.* New York: Alfred A. Knopf, 1994. Nuland offers a candid and compassionate examination of the physical and emotional processes of death, demystifying the medical realities of how life ends while reflecting on the dignity and complexity of dying.

Rumi. *The Essential Rumi.* Translated by Coleman Barks. New York: HarperCollins, 1995. This is a collection of Rumi's inimitable and lyrical poetry, offering spiritual insights on love, longing, and the mystical experience of union with the divine. Barks's translations have been widely praised for capturing the spiritual essence and emotional depth of Rumi's work. The excerpt is from the poem, *Story Water.*

Easwaran, Eknath. *The Upanishads.* Tomales, CA: Nilgiri Press, 2007. Easwaran's version offers a clear and accessible translation of these ancient Hindu spiritual texts, exploring profound philosophical concepts such as the nature of reality, the self, and the ultimate unity of all existence.

Easwaran, Eknath. *The Bhagavad Gita*. Tomales, CA: Nilgiri Press, 2007. Easwaran's accessible translation presents the *Bhagavad Gita* in clear, poetic prose, and commentary for applying its wisdom to modern life.

Grof, Stanislav. *The Way of the Psychonaut: Encyclopedia for Inner Journeys*. Volume 1. Santa Cruz, CA: Multidisciplinary Association for Psychedelic Studies, 2019. Grof's seminal two-volume work serves as an in-depth guide to exploring human consciousness through non-ordinary states, including methods like Holotropic Breathwork and psychedelic therapy.

Yogananda, Paramahansa. *Autobiography of a Yogi*. 1946. Reprint, Los Angeles: Self-Realization Fellowship, 1998.

Robinson, Marilynne. *Gilead*. New York: Farrar, Straus and Giroux, 2004. This Pulitzer Prize-winning novel is a series of meditations on faith, grace, and the complexities of human relationships.

Andrew Newberg, M.D., is widely known for his pioneering research focused on the development of neurotransmitter tracers for the evaluation of religiosity, to which he refers to as "neurotheology." Refer to *Sense of Mind* podcast April 15, 2022: https://www.youtube.com/watch?v=9KmWbvVOT0E

Aurobindo, Sri, and The Mother. *The Psychic Being: Soul, Its Nature, Mission, and Evolution*. Twin Lakes, WI: Lotus Press, 1990. The authors explore the concept of the soul's evolution, focusing on the inner spiritual self, its mission, and its role in human growth and divine realization and introduce the term *psychic being* to describe immobile and silent presence behind ordinary mental, vital and physical consciousness.

Schwartz, Robert. *Your Soul's Plan: Discovering the Real Meaning of the Life You Planned Before You Were Born*. Charlottesville, VA: North Atlantic Books, 2009; and, Schwartz, Robert. *Your Soul's Gift: The Healing Power of the Life You Planned Before You Were*

Born. Charlottesville, VA: North Atlantic Books, 2012. Schwartz explores the idea that souls plan significant life challenges before birth to foster ontological and current-life spiritual growth. Using a thorough phenomenological process with in-depth case studies and interviews of individuals who have accessed their pre-birth plans through hypnosis and past life regression, Schwartz reveals several grounded insights into the purposefulness behind life's difficulties as well, suggests over-arching purpose for life in the body.

Laurence, Tim. *The Hoffman Process: The World-Famous Technique That Empowers You to Forgive Your Past, Heal Your Present, and Transform Your Future*. New York: Bantam, 2003. Laurence outlines the transformative psychological and spiritual program that helps individuals resolve emotional issues from their past, fostering self-awareness and healing through compassion, forgiveness, and free-will.

Chapter Six

Nelson, Annabelle. *Archetypal Imagery and the Spirit Self: Techniques for Coaches and Therapists* (2014) provides a practical guide for using archetypal imagery as a tool for emotional and spiritual healing. Nelson offers techniques for coaches and therapists seeking to integrate creative and spiritual methods into their practice to support clients' growth and well-being.

Ring, Kenneth, and Evelyn Elsaesser Valarino. *Lessons from the Light: What We Can Learn from the Near-Death Experience*. Needham, MA: Moment Point Press, 1998. Exploration and insights gained from near-death experiences (NDEs) and how these profound experiences can offer lessons on life, death, and spiritual growth from a foremost leader in NDE research and publication.

Twist, Lynne. *Living a Committed Life: Finding Freedom and Fulfillment in a Purpose Larger Than Yourself*. Oakland, CA: Berrett-Koehler Publishers, 2022.

Chapter Seven

Bohm, David. *Wholeness and the Implicate Order*. London: Routledge, 1980. Bohm presents his theory of the universe as an interconnected whole, introducing the concept of the "implicate order" where all things are enfolded and interconnected, contrasting with the "explicate order" of separated objects in everyday experience.

Teilhard de Chardin, Pierre. *The Phenomenon of Man*. New York: Harper & Row, 1959. de Chardin blends science and theology to propose a vision of evolution as a process leading toward increasing complexity and consciousness, ultimately culminating in the spiritual unification of humanity in what he calls the "Omega Point."

Campbell, Joseph, and Bill Moyers. *The Power of Myth*. New York: Doubleday, 1988. The quote is attributed to Campbell from his interviews in the 1988 PBS series *The Power of Myth* with Bill Moyers, where Campbell popularized the idea of "following your bliss" as a way to align with your true purpose and discover unexpected opportunities.

Campbell, Joseph. *The Hero with a Thousand Faces*. 2nd ed. Princeton: Princeton University Press, 1968; Campbell explores the concept of the monomyth or *hero's journey*, a universal pattern found in myths across cultures, illustrating how heroes undergo a cycle of departure, initiation, and return in their quest for transformation.

Chapter Eight

Carroll, Lewis. *Alice's Adventures in Wonderland*. New York: Bantam Books, 1984. Published originally in 1865, this is whimsical tale centers on a young girl's journey through a fantastical world, where she encounters a series of curious and bizarre characters, exploring themes of identity, logic, and absurdity in a dreamlike narrative.

Frankl, Viktor E. *Man's Search for Meaning*. Boston: Beacon Press, 2006. Frankl openly reflects on extreme experiences, and the meaning he derived from them, as a Holocaust survivor and psychiatrist, presenting his theory of logotherapy, which emphasizes the human drive to find meaning in life, even in the face of suffering.

Kuhn, Thomas S. *The Structure of Scientific Revolutions*. 2nd ed. Chicago: University of Chicago Press, 1970. Kuhn's work has had profound significance across multiple disciplines, fundamentally reshaping our understanding of how scientific knowledge evolves. His concept of *paradigm shifts* challenged the previously dominant view of scientific progress as a steady, cumulative process.

Karcher, Stephen. *I Ching: The Classic Chinese Oracle of Change*. New York: St. Martin's Press, 2002. This is a scholarly and accessible interpretation of the ancient Chinese divination text, blending traditional wisdom with modern insights.

Chapter Nine

Daumal, René. *Mount Analogue: A Novel of Symbolically Authentic Non-Euclidean Adventures in Mountain Climbing*. Translated by Roger Shattuck. New York: Overlook Press, 1974; English translation by Roger Shattuck. Daumal's writing is a spiritual and allegorical exploration of life and transcendence, using the metaphor of mountain climbing to symbolize the journey toward higher understanding.

Emerson, Ralph Waldo. *The Spiritual Emerson: Essential Writings*. Edited by David M. Robinson. Boston: Beacon Press, 2003. This quote is from Emerson's essay "Compensations," which is part of his collection *Essays: First Series*, published in 1841.

Chapter Ten

Louise, Regina. *Permission Granted: Kick-Ass Strategies to Bootstrap Your Way to Unconditional Self-Love*. Novato, CA:

New World Library, 2021. Speaker, teacher, coach and author offers life lessons, practical strategies, and motivational advice for readers to embrace self-love, overcome self-doubt, and live unapologetically, encouraging a deep sense of personal empowerment and self-worth.

hooks, bell. *All About Love: New Visions*. New York: William Morrow & Company, 2000. Influential author, feminist theorist, and social activist, hooks best known for her groundbreaking work on race, gender, and class, challenges conventional ideas of love, advocating for a redefinition of love rooted in care, respect, and emotional growth, while critiquing how societal dysfunctions hinder our ability to truly experience and offer love.

Palmer, Parker J. *On the Brink of Everything: Grace, Gravity, and Getting Old*. Oakland: Berrett-Koehler Publishers, 2018. A reflective and insightful exploration of aging, offering meditations on life's journey as one nears its later stages. Palmer encourages readers of all ages to embrace life with authenticity and wisdom, engaging deeply with the world as time passes.

Garrity, Robert M. "St. Bernard on the Importance of Authentic Self-Love." *Heythrop Journal* 61, no. 1 (2020): 1–14. The article focuses on the concept of graced self-love in St. Bernard of Clairvaux's spiritual theology, exploring the reasons behind this emphasis, the practical benefits of authentic self-love, and the theological and mystical dimensions of Bernard's thought.

Neff, Kristin. *Self-Compassion: The Proven Power of Being Kind to Yourself*. New York: HarperCollins, 2011. A pioneer researcher and leading expert on self-compassion, Neff explores the concept of self-compassion and provides empirical findings and practical tools for developing kindness and understanding toward oneself to foster emotional well-being and resilience.

Chapter Twelve

Angelou, Maya. *SuperSoul Sunday.* Oprah Winfrey Network, 2013. https://youtu.be/gwuAntPHGVM?feature=shared.

Lusseyran, Jacques. *And There Was Light: The Extraordinary Memoir of a Blind Hero of the French Resistance in World War II.* Translated by Elizabeth R. Cameron. Novato, CA: New World Library, 2014.

Duprée, Ulrich E. *Ho'oponopono: The Hawaiian Forgiveness Ritual as the Key to Your Life's Fulfillment.* 2nd ed. London: Earthdancer Books, 2012. This little book explains the ancient Hawaiian practice of Ho'oponopono, focusing on its application for healing, reconciliation, and personal transformation—in a simple way that's easy to adopt and use.

Chapter Thirteen

Emerson, Ralph Waldo. *The Spiritual Emerson: Essential Writings.* Edited by David M. Robinson. Boston: Beacon Press, 2003. This quote is from Emerson's essay "Circles," which is part of his collection *Essays: First Series*, published in 1841.

Lamott, Anne. *Somehow: Thoughts on Love.* New York: Riverhead Books, 2024. This often quirky and insightful exploration, is a reminder of the many surprising manifestations of love and in its transformative and complex forms that shape our lives.

MANTRA
BOOKS

EASTERN RELIGION & PHILOSOPHY

We publish books on Eastern religions and philosophies. Books that aim to inform and explore the various traditions that began in the East and have migrated West.
If you have enjoyed this book, why not tell other readers by posting a review on your preferred book site.

Recent Bestsellers from MANTRA BOOKS Are:

The Way Things Are
A Living Approach to Buddhism
Lama Ole Nydahl
An introduction to the teachings of the Buddha, and how to make use of these teachings in everyday life.
Paperback: 978-1-84694-042-2 ebook: 978-1-78099-845-9

Back to the Truth
5000 Years of Advaita
Dennis Waite
A demystifying guide to Advaita for both those new to, and those
familiar with this ancient, non-dualist philosophy from India.
Paperback: 978-1-90504-761-1 ebook: 978-184694-624-0

Shinto: A celebration of Life
Aidan Rankin
Introducing a gentle but powerful spiritual pathway reconnecting
humanity with Great Nature and arming all aspects of life.
Paperback: 978-1-84694-438-3 ebook: 978-1-84694-738-4

In the Light of Meditation
Mike George
A comprehensive introduction to the practice of meditation and the spiritual principles behind it. A 10 lesson meditation programme with CD and internet support.
Paperback: 978-1-90381-661-5

The 7 Levels of Wisdom
Mónica Esgueva
A straightforward and compelling approach on how to reach the highest levels of consciousness, wisdom, and inner peace.
Paperback: 978-1-80341-470-6 ebook: 978-1-80341-471-3

Compassion Based Living Course
Heather Regan-Addis and Choden
A practical guide to living a compassionate life.
Paperback: 978-1-80341-676-2 ebook: 978-1-80341-709-7

The Sacred Gathas of Zarathushtra & the Old Avestan Canon
Pablo Vazquez
The ancient and mystical poetry of Zarathushtra and the first Zoroastrians: Now accessible to the public in a modern translation.
Paperback: 978-1-78535-961-3 ebook: 978-1-78535-962-0

Radiant Bliss
Sue Bushell
Embrace Your Journey: Unfolding Peace, Power, and Purpose Through Yoga
Paperback: 978-1-80341-818-6 ebook: 978-1-80341-822-3

Ordinary Women, Extraordinary Wisdom
Rita Marie Robinson
The Feminine Face of Awakening
A collection of intimate conversations with female spiritual teachers who live like ordinary women, but are engaged with their true natures.
Paperback: 978-1-84694-068-2 ebook: 978-1-78099-908-1

The Riddle of Alchemy
Paul Kiritsis
What is alchemy, exactly? Is there any empirical truth to ancient speculative pursuits toward metallic transmutation? How does alchemy intersect with Western mind sciences and science in general?
Paperback: 978-1-80341-637-3 ebook: 978-1-80341-688-5

Readers of ebooks can buy or view any of these bestsellers by clicking on the live link in the title. Most titles are published in paperback and as an ebook. Paperbacks are available in traditional bookshops. Both print and ebook formats are available online.

Find more titles and sign up to our readers' newsletter at www.collectiveinkbooks.com/mind-body-spirit. Follow us on Facebook at facebook.com/OBooks and Twitter at twitter.com/obooks